GW00370937

Short Cuts to glory

Short Cuts to glory

The easy beginner's guide
for Australian cooks
with Matt Okine

echo

In association with PQ Blackwell

Contents

Introduction

I grew up around food: my dad, the infamous Daddy Mack, would cook up a storm for his African Club night in Brisbane on a regular basis. At a young age I was familiar with the sight of stews bubbling away on the stovetop, smoke billowing from the hibachi and the smell of black-eyed beans and peanut soup filling the house.

When I first moved out of home, however, my diet consisted almost entirely of packet noodles, canned tuna and toasted cheese sandwiches (not to mention copious amounts of cask wine . . . but that's a story for a different book). When I was gifted an outdoor barbecue by a neighbour, suddenly a fondness for food was ignited (pun intended) and I soon realised that a love of cooking must run in the family.

When you're young and unemployed (except for your part-time job in a call centre), meal-making isn't just a task, it's an event! Something to look forward to for your entire day. With all the time in the world and barely any of the money, you have to get creative. And through making the recipes in this book, I've come to realise that some of the most iconic dishes from around the globe were born from a similar creativity: consider the rustic Italian roots of a minestrone soup, or the seaside origins of Spain's most loved dish, paella.

Taking us from the harbourside home of Monday Morning Cooking Club, who share a super-simple shortcut for smashed potatoes, to the fiery kitchen at Bondi's Icebergs, where Monty Koludrovic masters

a bowl of mussels, *Short Cuts to Glory* is all about cutting the fat (again, pun intended) from your kitchen faffing and getting down to the nitty-gritty: good, healthy meals, prepared quickly, that look amazing and leave you with a bunch of budget remaining in your back pocket.

Whether you are a knife-wielding novice or a meal-making maestro, this book is for you. It's about bringing world-class technique to trusted homemade favourites, and giving you the secrets to recipes you'll use for life! It's about bringing the café to your kitchen when you're too lazy (or hungover) to venture out, or impressing that special someone on a date night. It's about feeding the mouths of millions when you go a little bit too hyper on the dinner-party invites, or just treating yourself to something quick and simple (but still worthy of an Instagram pic) when you're home alone after a massive day's work.

But the main thing I have learnt from all the chefs on this long journey of many shortcuts is: have fun! The precise measurements for each and every recipe are not binding in a court of law, and it will not cause the world to cave in and the fiery caverns of hell to open up should you miss a gram of something here or there. Be brave, take risks and trust your tongue, for not every tastebud is the same, and sometimes you just don't have smoked paprika in the cupboard.

Bon appétit, legend!

Matt Okine
Master presenter, apprentice chef

Kitchen 101

Kitchen 101:
Cooktops

with Alice Zaslavsky

Unless you only ever pour boiling water over a cup of noodles, the cooktop is the one piece of kitchen equipment you'll be using 95 per cent of the time.

So, how do you actually use one?

How you use your cooktop depends on whether you have a gas or electric one. It does take practice to get to know your cooktop and to understand which burner or hob is better for which task. Some cooktops have special little idiosyncrasies that you will only learn about the more you use them.

Gas

Most gas cooktops now have automatic ignition. To turn a burner on, turn the dial a little way on and depress the button. The ignition spark will make little clicks and after just a few seconds the gas will light. Adjust the flame to high or low, as you need. If there is no automatic ignition, turn the dial a little way on and use the ignition button — on a freestanding oven this is sometimes located on the left-hand side.

If you have to use a match, do so. Turn the gas on a little way and bring the lighted match in from one side of the burner and just above it — don't try to light it over the top. Better still, you can get a long clicker lighter — much safer.

Always check that the flame is actually on. If the gas doesn't light quickly, turn the dial back to zero and check that the metal caps on the burners are sitting correctly in place before trying again.

Electric and ceramic

Turning on your electric cooktop is easy — just turn the dial! However, it can be hard to tell if it's on, as there are no visual signs of heat (unless it's a ceramic cooktop, which will glow red). Choose your burner carefully from the burner options — the little dots most electric cooktops use can be very confusing. Some cooktops have lights that come on if the burner is hot. If you're not sure whether a burner is on or not, hold your hand at least 50 cm above the cooktop to feel for the heat — never touch a burner.

Some temperature indicators have a small flame and a large flame, some have knobs that indicate low and high, and some use numbers as a guide (sometimes 1-6, and sometimes 1-10). Induction cooktops use digital readings.

Remember to turn the cooktop off after you've finished cooking.

What's the main difference between gas and electric?

Gas is very fast and visual. Electric and ceramic cooktops are much slower to heat up and cool down. If your milk is starting to boil over, you can turn gas down pretty much instantly but for the others you need to quickly move the pot off the hotspot.

Why are there different-sized burners?

The different sizes of burner accommodate different-sized pots with large and small quantities of foods to be cooked. Also, some cooking methods and foods require super-high heat and some super-low heat. The bigger the burner, the higher it can heat.

Make sure that your pot or pan is bigger than the burner — there is nothing worse than the smell of a burning saucepan handle, and you can also hurt yourself when picking up a pan by a hot handle.

How long do I preheat for?

If you need to preheat your pan or wok, when cooking a steak or a stir-fry, for example, place your pan on the largest burner over a high heat. Hover your hand about 5 cm from the pan until you feel the heat radiating up. You should hear a sizzle when you add the food.

You can also see the heat shimmering above the pan when it gets screaming hot.

What does medium-high actually mean?

This means crank the heat up to high and then turn it down slightly.

How can I stop things from burning?

Be vigilant — use a timer, especially when cooking rice. Make sure you use good-quality pots and pans (see page 20). Use all of your senses (including your sixth sense!) as this helps enormously when cooking.

Kitchen 101:
Ovens

with Alice Zaslavsky

From roasting a chook or cooking a casserole to baking brownies or making a pavlova, the oven is a useful tool, but it can be quite daunting if you don't know how to use it. All ovens work slightly differently — some cook hotter than others, for example — so it pays to get to know your oven and its idiosyncrasies well.

What's the difference between baking and roasting?

Baking applies to soft, doughy ingredients that are going to solidify in the oven, such as breads, cakes, cookies and pastry. Roasting applies to solid foods, such as meat and vegetables. Both methods use the same technique: cooking with dry heat.

Why does a gas oven cook differently from an electric one?

The gas comes on at the bottom of the oven, and therefore the heat rises from there — this makes the heat in a gas oven harder to control. An electric oven (which is preferable) has a top and a bottom element, and usually a fan to distribute the heat evenly.

What's the deal with low, medium and high oven temperatures?

A low temperature is around 140-150°C and is used for things like casseroles and stews. A moderate or medium temperature is around 170-190°C and is used for standard roasting and baking (e.g. cakes, pastry, meat and vegetables). A hot or high temperature is around 200-220°C and is used for roasting large cuts of meat. Most recipes will specify a temperature as a guide, but you should get to know your oven — some ovens, especially older ones, tend to fluctuate 10°C either side of the temperature you set. Some ovens also have hotspots. When you are getting to know your oven, check regularly — especially with baking — until you have a feel for how it works.

How do I preheat?

Preheating the oven is essential when baking cakes and biscuits, and always advisable. Turn your oven on to the desired temperature a little ahead of time, then wait for the indicator light to switch off — this shows that the oven has reached temperature. It should take about 5-10 minutes, depending on your oven.

When do I use fan-forced?

If you are cooking a few dishes on several levels in your oven, use fan-forced. The fan circulates the air around the oven so that everything cooks more evenly. To convert conventional oven temperatures to fan-forced temperatures, reduce by 20°C (e.g. 180°C conventional = 160°C fan-forced).

If you don't have a fan-forced option on your oven, the shelf that you use becomes more important (see right).

Which shelf do I use?

Ovens typically come with two oven racks, which you can place in one of several 'shelf' positions in the oven. If your recipe doesn't specify a shelf height, use the following guide:

Use the **bottom shelf** if you are roasting a chicken or a leg of lamb, or cooking a casserole.

The **middle shelf** is best for baking cakes and biscuits. However, scones go in closer to the top shelf — heat rises to the top, and scones are better suited to this spot as they require a short burst of high heat.

The **top shelf** is reserved for grilling.

What do all the symbols on my oven mean?

The symbols on different ovens vary in style, but are mostly similar in what they depict. Not all ovens have all of the functions, but the common ones are outlined below.

Bake/convection (heat from the top and bottom elements) is used for baking and roasting. Typical symbol: a box with a horizontal line at the top and the bottom.

Fan-forced is used for roasting and baking on multiple levels, and is best suited to dishes requiring a temperature below 180°C. Typical symbol: a box with a horizontal line top and bottom and a fan shape in the middle.

Grill is used for cooking items on one side at a time. Typical symbol: a box with a zigzag at the top.

Fan-grill circulates air from the top element, and grills more evenly and quickly than a grill alone. Typical symbol: a box with a zigzag at the top and a fan shape below.

Defrost (no heat) is to be avoided, as it's not great for food safety! It's better to defrost food in the fridge or the microwave. Typical symbol: a box with no lines inside, just a fan shape, or a dripping snowflake.

Oven light allows you to see inside the oven without opening the door, which is particularly useful when baking, as baked goods can be very sensitive to fluctuating temperature. Typical symbol: a box with a light bulb shape inside.

Bottom element only is good for baking pies and frozen meals. Typical symbol: a box with a horizontal line just at the bottom.

Kitchen 101:
Kitchen Tools

with Sarah Glover

Here is a list of basic kitchen tools to get you started — arranged in order of what you should aim to buy first. You'll find some of these in the supermarket, but it's best to go to a shop that specialises in home- and kitchenware.

TIP
Asian grocers, op shops and restaurant-supply stores can also be a treasure trove of affordable kitchen utensils — just go in and have a look around.

Chopping board

Besides size, it's also important to consider what material your chopping boards are made from.

Wooden boards are quite durable and will also be kinder to your knives — boards are usually easier to replace than knives. The downside is that raw wood absorbs moisture and you run the risk of bacteria growing inside your board where you can't really sanitise it thoroughly. They are also prone to warping if not taken care of properly, and should be washed by hand. Prices start from about $10–$15 for a 30 cm x 20 cm wooden chopping board.

Plastic boards are generally quite cheap and easy to replace, and the different colours available mean that you can have colour-coded boards for meat, fish, poultry, veg and dairy if you so desire. Unfortunately they are fairly harsh on your knives and wear fairly quickly. Plastic boards may also warp over time if you wash them in the dishwasher. Prices start from about $4 for a 30 cm x 20 cm chopping board.

① **Metal or silicone square-end fish slice/turner**

An all-rounder in terms of frying, the square-end fish slice (also known as a turner) has a wide, flat surface, which allows you to flip meat, fish, eggs and pancakes with ease. When choosing your fish slice, consider the frying pan you'll be using. Metal fish slices don't play well with non-stick coatings because they scratch, so silicone can be a really good option. However, silicone fish slicers are not as sturdy as the metal ones. Prices start from $3.

② **Locking tongs**

Tongs are great for lifting or turning large items, and you can use the scooped ends to serve up smaller items like roasted vegetables. They come with or without silicone ends. Plain metal tongs are the best for beginners, because the silicone tips often don't have as much grip — and food slipping back into hot oil does not make for the most enjoyable experience! Prices start from about $3 for a large pair of tongs at mass retailers.

③ **Wooden spoon**

The classic wooden spoon is a fantastic tool for making both sweet and savoury dishes, and the wood won't scratch your non-stick surfaces. You can get a basic one for as little as $1 in restaurant-supply stores or $2 at mass retailers.

④ **Vegetable peeler**

These come in two general shapes — the conventional, straight vegetable peeler with a straight-edged blade to the side, or a Y-shaped 'speed peeler' with the straight-edged blade perpendicular to the handle. They can be used to (surprise!) peel your vegetables and to create 'noodles' from veggies such as cucumbers, carrots and zucchinis. You can also use a peeler to create cheese or chocolate shavings. Prices start at $2 for a basic plastic straight-edged peeler.

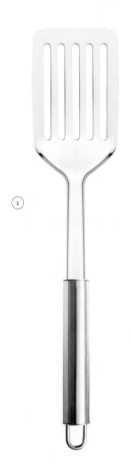

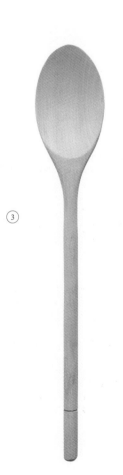

① Can opener

Used to open cans (and, if you're into life hacks, some rigid plastic packaging, too), can openers are generally either electric or manual (as pictured below). Some open the can from the side and others from the top — it's all a matter of preference. Prices start from $5 for a manual metal can opener.

② Colander/sieve

These are used mostly to drain water or liquids from solids — anything from washing rice or veggies to draining canned beans or cooked pasta. Colanders (as pictured below) typically have a handle each side and the holes are quite large; sieves have a single handle and are made of wire mesh. A metal-handled sieve is very handy for quick-blanching green veggies or noodles by dipping them in boiling water. Prices start from $5 for a metal colander or $3 for a plastic-handled sieve.

③ Measuring cups & spoons

Measuring cups and spoons differ from country to country. Australian cups are 250 ml each and our tablespoon measures 20 ml. American cups are 240 ml each and their tablespoon is 15 ml. Always check the origin of your recipe so that you can adjust your measurements where needed. Prices start from $2 for a set of plastic/silicone cups or a set of metal spoons. You can also get a plastic 600 ml measuring jug for about $3, which has measurements up the side in 20 ml increments.

④ General-purpose kitchen scissors

These are a bit hardier than your office stationery scissors. They often feature one serrated edge to keep them cutting for longer. You can use them for a variety of purposes, from butterflying a chicken to snipping herbs. Prices start from $3 for a basic pair.

⑤

Grater

Graters allow you to get a different texture from otherwise familiar ingredients, like carrots, cheese, chocolate, etc. They come in different grades and thicknesses. Choose a grater that has a selection of grating and slicing holes. Prices start from $3 for a basic grater.

⑥

Whisk

The tines of a whisk are used to aerate things like eggs or batter. In many instances you could also use a fork. Prices start at $5 for a stainless-steel whisk.

⑦

Slotted spoon

This is usually used to lift out smallish solids, like poached eggs, from a pot of hot liquid. Prices start from $5 for a stainless-steel slotted spoon or $3 for a silicone one.

⑧

Potato masher

These are made for mashing potatoes, but will also lightly crush par-boiled baby potatoes to give them a crispy edge when roasting (see page 102). A metal potato masher can also be used to break up beef mince in the frying pan. Prices start from $2 for a plastic potato masher and $5 for a metal one. If you don't have a masher yet, you can use a fork.

⑤

⑥

⑦

⑧

TIP
Plastic containers help to keep your fridge and pantry organised, prevent pests (due to unsealed packages) and avoid food wastage.

Kitchen 101:
Frying Pans

with Jemma Whiteman

It may seem like there are a thousand different types of frying pans, but what's the best one for you? What you should buy depends on what you'll be cooking most often and on your budget.

What makes a good-quality pan?

With frying pans, as with many other things, there's a fine balance of price versus what you'll get — the material, coating (if any) and size will all affect the cost. In general, you're looking for a good weight to your pan and something that will last through all the cleaning and cooking you're going to put it through — especially if you're just learning how to cook. You also want something that will conduct/retain heat well, which usually means that it's a pan that won't bend when you apply pressure.

What's the first pan I should buy if I don't own any?

It's a good idea to get something that's versatile. A fairly wide (around 26-28 cm) high-sided pan is a good place to start — the height will allow you to do some stewing and the width will allow you to fry and get a good sear. The sides of the pan shouldn't be too high, though, as this can lead to stewing instead of frying. Bear in mind that many domestic electric cooktops don't recommend a larger size than 28 cm.

What about all the different materials?

All the materials commonly used in cookware have their own pros and cons.

Stainless-steel pans are the best all-rounders and are suitable for use on all cooktops. If the handles are stainless steel, the pan will be ovenproof and can double as a small roasting pan. On the downside, stainless-steel pans are a little heavier than most people are used to, and not the cheapest on the market.

Aluminium pans are the lightest and cheapest, and are widely available from major chain stores. However, they can have poor heat retention and they're prone to hotspots, so your food may cook inconsistently. Most aluminium pans have plastic handles, so are not oven-safe.

Copper pans have the best heat conductivity of the lot and are ovenproof as well. However, they are usually the most expensive and they can be a nightmare to clean.

Cast-iron pans are sturdy, with fantastic heat retention, and the temperatures they can achieve mean you can get an amazing sear on your meat. On the downside, they're pretty heavy and take a long time to heat up, which can be annoying if you're really hungry and just trying to fry an egg.

Recommendation: a 26 cm stainless-steel sauté pan (also known as a chef's pan), with a lid if possible. Expect to pay up to $50 for a durable pan that will take a little bit of abuse. If you can't afford that, buy a pan with some sort of quality guarantee, so that you can take it back to the shop and get a new one if it starts to wear early.

Lid or no lid?

Where possible, get a pan with a lid that fits. Glass lids are good because you can monitor how your food is cooking without lifting the lid. If your pan didn't come with a lid, you can buy one separately, or use aluminium foil for a quick option.

Is non-stick necessary?

Non-stick pans are useful when you're starting out, because you don't need to keep such a close eye on the food to make sure it's not sticking. There are a number of non-stick options on the market. The most common of these is **Polytetrafluoroethylene (PTFE), e.g. Teflon**. It's a bit controversial because earlier versions of this coating used a chemical that is toxic and, although it's been phased out, some stigma remains.

Pans with PTFE coating shouldn't be used over very high heat, so if you're cooking a lot at hotter temperatures, plain stainless steel is best.

What are the main types of frying pans?

 ①

Frying pan
A pan that is wide and very shallow is usually considered to be a frying pan. It's generally a good idea to err on the side of your pan being too wide, because that means more versatility and bang for your buck. A frying pan that's too small can lead to over-crowding, and your food will stew instead of frying.

 ②

Sauté pan/chef's pan
This is a wide pan with higher sides than a frying pan — height-wise, it looks somewhere between a frying pan and a saucepan. It's slightly more versatile than a straight frying pan as it allows you to stew and braise as well as fry. The width gives better evaporation than a saucepan, which can help to concentrate the flavours.

 ③

Wok
A frying pan with a rounded shape, high sides and (sometimes) a flat bottom for balance is a wok. Its large surface area makes it good for dishes that require fast cooking, such as stir-fries, but domestic cooktops are often not hot enough to fully utilise this feature.

Kitchen 101:
Pots & Pans

with Lillia McCabe

As a new cook, should you buy a complete set of pots and pans or get single ones? What are all the different pots and pans for anyway? Here's a guide to buying the right ones.

What makes a good pot?

A good pot will be sturdy and won't warp, and will preferably have a thick, heavy base for even heat distribution. Just as with frying pans, you'll want your pots to be as versatile as possible. Stainless-steel pots with welded or riveted steel handles and glass lids will enable you to go from stovetop to oven, which opens up so many more recipe possibilities.

What are the first pots and pans I should buy if I don't own any?

If you're starting out on a budget, get yourself two pans to begin with — a medium-sized (2-litre) aluminium saucepan (about $5–$10) and a larger (5-litre) aluminium stockpot (about $10–$15). These will allow you to do everything from boiling an egg to cooking a stew. If there's a well-priced set available or you've got some extra cash, add a small pan (about 1.4 litres; also in the $5–$10 range) to the list. The stockpot should come with a lid, but the smaller pans may or may not have lids included.

Stainless steel is usually recommended across the board, but most beginner recipes involving pots only require boiling or stewing, where even heat distribution isn't as important — aluminium is fine for this. If money is less of an issue, go with the same sizes but in stainless steel.

What about all the different materials?

All the materials commonly used in cookware have their own pros and cons. For a discussion of stainless steel versus aluminium, copper and cast iron, see pages 18-19. Pots and pans also come in ceramic and clay (earthenware), which are good options for those worried about metal leaching into their food. Ceramic pots retain heat well and are easy to clean, but they can be delicate and not all of them are recommended for gas cooktops. Clay pots are less delicate and are particularly good for recipes that require slow-cooking, but they can be bulky and difficult to handle.

Is non-stick necessary?

Pots come with all sorts of non-stick coatings, just like frying pans do. However, given that pots are usually used for very wet methods of cooking — stewing, boiling, poaching, simmering — non-stick coating is less important.

What are the main types of pots and pans?

'Pots and pans' come in all different shapes and sizes, each suited to different types of cooking. As you become more experienced, you can build up your collection based on how you like to cook.

Milk pan

Generally used to describe single-handled pots with a capacity of up to 1 litre, milk pans are the smallest pans of the lot (10-15 cm), and are so called because they were originally just used to heat milk. Use one of these when boiling eggs or cooking rice for one.

Saucepan

A saucepan is generally any pot with a single handle, usually up to a capacity of 2.5 litres (because you wouldn't be able to easily handle much more using just one hand). The 'saucepan' category also encompasses the milk pan.

Stockpot

A stockpot is usually quite large — commercial pots can easily be up to 20 litres. They usually have two handles, because of the large capacity, and generally come with a lid.

Dutch oven

Generally oval in shape, Dutch ovens are also heavy (made from coated cast iron, ceramic or clay) and come with a matching lid. They are fantastic for stove-to-oven use (mostly due to the materials they're made of), and the shape and good heat retention mean that you can also use them to create fairly artisanal-looking bread loaves in a domestic oven.

Casserole dish

These usually come in two shapes — round or rectangular — and are made out of coated cast iron, ceramic or glass. Some are fairly shallow (crossing the line between a pot and a baking dish — see page 23). The lighter versions are easier to handle than Dutch ovens, but still give you a good amount of heat retention for oven-cooked dishes.

Should I preheat my pots?

Preheating will help you achieve a good sear, so is only necessary if you are looking to brown vegetables or meat.

What about cleaning?

Most pots will respond well to cleaning with warm, soapy water (if you have non-stick pots, be especially careful not to scratch them). Many modern pots can be cleaned in the dishwasher, but check the cleaning instructions when buying.

An exception to this general rule are uncoated cast-iron pots and pans — these require cleaning with heat and salt to maintain the seasoning.

Kitchen 101:
Trays, Tins & Dishes

with Sarah Glover

There is a huge range of trays, tins, pans and dishes available for roasting and baking in (or on). They all come in handy, but what's the best to buy on a budget when starting to cook?

A tray is a tray is a tray, right?

Well, no. It's not just the width and length that matter, but the depth as well. A flatter tray (a baking sheet) allows better heat circulation and is good for baking things like cookies. A deeper tray (a roasting tray) lets larger items cook through without losing too much moisture, and also allows for delicious juices to accumulate without spilling over. A deeper tray also allows you to bake sheet cakes, which makes it more versatile than a baking sheet.

What should I buy to start off with?

A roasting tray should be the first thing on your shopping list — this will allow you to bake cakes and cookies as well as roast your Sunday dinner. Bonus points if it includes a roasting rack. Follow this up with a brownie pan for cooking smaller items, and then a baking sheet (cookie tray).

Once you've got started, you can build up your trays, tins and dishes depending on what you like to cook.

What size tray should I get?

Short answer: measure your oven. There's nothing worse than buying a tray because it 'looks all right' and then coming home only to realise that it won't fit in your oven (and different makes and styles of oven are different shapes). A good trick is bringing one of your oven roasting racks to the shops with you so that you can make sure it will fit.

Why get a roasting rack?

If you can, get a roasting tray that also includes a roasting rack (also sometimes called a trivet). These are removable racks that you can use to elevate your meat above your veggies to allow more even heat circulation. If you get a roasting tray with a flat roasting rack (as opposed to a V-shaped one), you can also use it as a cake rack and trivet to keep hot pans off your benchtop.

What about all the different materials?

For a beginner, aluminium trays are generally the cheapest, lightest and easiest to buy. A 35 cm x 24 cm x 6 cm aluminium roasting tray with a roasting rack will set you back about $10. Stainless steel is a good all-round material and will last through years of scrubbing, but is a little more expensive at around $20. Glass and ceramic trays are popular with those who are concerned about metal leaching into their food, but they can be more delicate than metal. If you want to use glass, it will cost about $13 for a comparable tray; ceramic is a bit pricier at around $30.

Is non-stick necessary?

Most trays and tins are available with a non-stick coating, but this isn't particularly essential as you can use (non-stick) baking paper and/or aluminium foil to line the tin or tray. This has two purposes — it stops the food sticking to the tray, and it's easier to clean your tray afterwards.

What are the main types of trays, tins and dishes?

Here is a brief outline of the different types.

Roasting tray
This is a wide, deep tray that is rectangular in shape. They are generally wide and long enough to hold an entire lamb leg roast, and are at least 3 cm deep. A common size is about 35 cm x 24 cm x 6 cm.

Brownie pan
This pan measures about 27 cm x 17.5 cm x 3 cm, and is usually used for brownies (naturally) and cakes. It looks like a mini roasting tray, and can also be used for things like roasting small sweet potatoes whole for two people.

Slice pan
A slice pan measures 29 cm x 19 cm x 3 cm and is used predominately for making slices, but is really just a shallower, wider brownie pan.

Baking sheet
Also known as a cookie sheet, this is a wide, flat tray that looks like a shallow version of a roasting tray. The negligible (sometimes non-existent) sides allow maximum heat circulation, so that items like cookies will bake more evenly. They're also very handy as a base to stand silicone moulds and bakeware on.

Baking dish
If your recipe just calls for a baking dish (as opposed to, say, an 'aluminium baking dish') this usually means something made of ceramic or glass. Baking dishes can look a little like a roasting tray but are often smaller and can also be round.

Cake tin
These come in all shapes and sizes — round, square, rectangular, etc. They have high sides (at least 5 cm), which means that you have plenty of room for your cake to rise.

Loose-based tin
The base of this baking tin isn't secured to the sides (it sits inside on a rim). Loose-based tins are mainly used for anything that has a crust, such as pies and tarts, as the unsecured base can otherwise allow batter to leak out.

Springform tin
The sides of these tins are secured by a spring-loaded mechanism, allowing cakes and tarts to be removed easily. Once the sides are locked in, the base is tightly secured.

Loaf pan
These are shaped like a loaf of bread, and are usually used for bread-making: banana bread, white bread, etc. They can also be used for meat loaf or to set semifreddos in.

Silicone mould
These come in all shapes and sizes, just like cake tins, but are called 'moulds' because they're made of silicone. They are fantastically non-stick, making cake removal a breeze, but they are also fairly poor conductors of heat. Cakes, breads, etc. baked in a silicone mould won't brown as well up the sides and on the bottom.

Kitchen 101:
Knives

with Mitch Orr

Forget all those expensive, fancy knife blocks with nine knives stacked in them — there are only three knives you'll ever need for cooking. Here we explain what to look for in a basic knife, how much to spend and what each knife is used for.

What makes a good knife?

Knives vary greatly in quality. Most modern knives are made of stainless steel, and the best come from Japan or Germany. German knives tend to be heavier and thicker, are very sturdy and last longer, but can feel a little more clumsy than their more delicate Japanese counterparts. Japanese knives are usually thinner and sharper, making them great for finer cutting work, but they also have a tendency to chip easily and require more care. Both Japanese and European knives are quite expensive ($100–$300 for a knife), so if you are looking at a more affordable price point, you can get a basic chef's knife for $6–$10. Just make sure that the blade is sharp and the metal is sturdy enough that it doesn't bow with light pressure.

What's the best way to sharpen a knife?

To keep knives sharp, you need a honing steel, which is a bit like a nail file for knives. Hold the blade on a 45° angle and drag it quickly across the fibres of the honing steel.

You can also get knives professionally sharpened. Some butchers provide this service for a good price.

HONING STEEL

What knives do I need to buy?

To start off any kitchen, all you need are a paring knife, a long serrated knife and a chef's knife.

Paring knife

This small knife (7–8 cm blade) is great for detailed work. It can be very cumbersome — not to mention dangerous! — to try to core a tomato with a big chef's knife, and this is where the paring knife really comes in handy. From coring fruit to peeling vegetables, it complements the bigger chef's knife.

Serrated knife

Usually, both chef's and paring knives come with a straight rather than a serrated blade, which — no matter how sharp the knife — can squash rather than cut certain softer foods. A good-quality serrated knife (10–17 cm blade) fixes this issue. It makes short work of foods like ripe tomatoes, eggplant, crusty breads and cakes, and never really needs to get sharpened, as the teeth do most of the work.

Chef's knife

This wide knife with a slightly curved blade and a fine tip is the workhorse of any kitchen. They come in varying lengths — from 12 cm to 23 cm blade length, not including the handle. Choose one that allows you to manoeuvre freely (i.e. it doesn't feel too large for you to control) while still giving you the depth of cut to efficiently slice through a small melon.

Apart from the blade, which parts of the knife are important when it comes to quality?

Tang

The tang is the join between the knife blade and its grip. A full tang is a single piece of metal that extends from the tip of the blade all the way to the base of the grip, and has usually been riveted into the grip, leaving the metal spine showing. This provides the most stability, as putting repeated stress on a short tang with a plastic handle can cause the join to weaken and be dangerous. However, there are many affordable knives with a half tang that are also very functional in the kitchen.

Grip

The grip is the handle of the knife. The first thing to think about is whether the knife is comfortable for you to hold — a too-small or a too-large grip can cause the knife to slip while you are chopping and could potentially be very dangerous. The second thing is whether you'll be able to hold the knife securely with damp hands. While you should never use a knife with wet hands, damp hands are somewhat unavoidable — especially if you're practising good hygiene and washing those mitts!

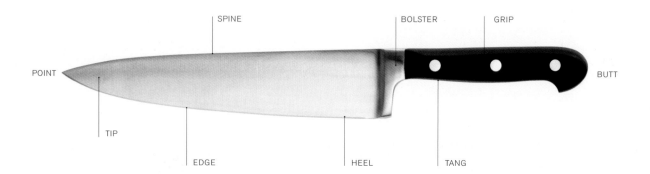

How should I care for my knife?

Washing

Knives should never be put in the dishwasher, as the vigorous wash cycle can cause the knives to get knocked around and the blade to get chipped. To clean your knife, simply wash it with a soft scourer (don't bother with the non-scratch scourers, as you sometimes need a little bit of help getting stuck-on bits of food off) under warm/hot water. Leave it to air dry — or dry it with a cloth — before storing.

 Safety note: *never leave a knife in a sink full of water — the knife can get obscured and create a dangerous situation for an unwitting person reaching in do the dishes!*

Storing

Knives in a drawer should be stored securely so that they move as little as possible when the drawer is opened and closed during the day. Unnecessary movement can chip or blunt a knife. Depending on the quality of the knife you've bought, this means that you'll either have to sharpen it or buy a new knife before its time. Knife blocks, drawer holders or a simple cover work very well.

What about all the other different types of knives?

Other types of knives can be useful in particular situations if you do want to expand your collection.

(1)

Boning knife
A mid-length, narrow, rigid knife that is used to bone out meat. The small tip makes it easy to cut around joints and through cartilage.

(2)

Filleting knife
Usually used for fish, this has a long, flexible, narrow blade that allows you to make quick work of getting fillets off a whole fish, or removing the skin off a side of fish.

(3)

Carving knife
Carving knives usually have long, straight, narrow blades, allowing you to slice through large chunks of roast meats with ease. These are sometimes sold with a carving fork, which has long tines to secure the meat whilst cutting.

(4)

Santoku
The santoku is a close Japanese cousin to the European chef's knife, but is shorter and has a straight rather than a curved blade. They often have dimples on the side of the blade, to create air pockets between the knife and the food, and to allow the food to fall away onto the board instead of sticking to the knife.

Kitchen 101:
Knife Skills

with Alice Zaslavsky

Here we explain the three basic chopping techniques: rolling, tapping and cross chopping. Then we move on to slicing and dicing.

What do I need to get started?

Buy the best chef's knife that you can afford, and look after it properly (see page 26). Set up your station with your knife and chopping board. You can also place a damp cloth under your chopping board to stop it moving around.

How do I hold the knife?

You can either hold the knife by its handle, or use a **pinch grip**: pinch the area where the blade meets the handle between your thumb and forefinger and wrap your other fingers around the handle. With this grip, the knife is an extension of your hand, and you have good control.

What should I do with my non-knife hand?

Remember to keep the fingers of your non-knife hand away from the blade. Form them into a **bear claw**: tuck your fingertips underneath and keep your thumb behind your fingers.

What are the basic chopping techniques?

The three basic chopping techniques are as follows. If you only master one of these, make it the rolling motion.

Rolling

Practise with something long and flat like celery. Hold your knife up above the celery with the point tipped down to touch the chopping board. Chop through the celery as you move the knife back toward you and then forward, always keeping the point of the knife on the board. Up, back, forward and repeat. Follow the 3 Ps: practise, practise, practise.

Tapping

Practise with a carton of mushrooms. First create a flat surface for yourself by slicing the base off the mushroom and sitting it down on its flat surface (this is called building a bridge). Then chop through the mushroom as you tap the knife up and down against the board.

Cross chopping

Practise with a big bunch of herbs. Roll them into a tight bundle and roughly chop through, then scrape the herbs together into a pile. Holding the tip of the blade still with your non-knife hand, chop up and down through the herbs, moving your knife hand across the pile. Scrape the herbs back into a pile and repeat until your herbs are chopped finely.

Holding the tip of the blade gives you extra control for smaller, more finicky jobs.

The bear claw   Rolling   Cross chopping

What about slicing and dicing?

Once you've got your basic chopping techniques sorted, learning how to slice and dice is the next logical step at becoming a gun in the kitchen.

Slicing and dicing an onion
The most common thing you're going to be asked to dice in a recipe is an onion. First, create a flat surface by cutting the onion in half from root to tip. Peel off a layer of skin (a good trick is to use the peeled-back skin as a handle you can hold the onion by). Follow the natural lines of the onion to make your slices, but don't cut all the way to the root (leaving the root intact keeps the onion together and minimises the fumes that make you cry!).

Next, turn the onion away from you at 90° and slice through it again on a 45° angle. Hold the onion together with your non-knife hand, making even slices about 1 cm apart. Discard the root, or freeze it to use later in a vegetable stock.

Slicing and dicing a garlic clove
Slice the clove finely first, taking your time to cut really thin slices. Stack them up into a little tower of garlic slices, then cut fine slices through the tower, making tiny sticks or **batons**. Line them back up again and repeat to make fine dice. The same dicing technique can be applied to other vegetables like carrots and celery: make slices, then batons, then cubes. Alternatively, you can use the cross-chopping technique (see opposite).

Common dice sizes
The size of your dice is up to you, but the three basic sizes that you might see in recipes are small, medium and large. Whatever one you choose, it's important that your dice are all a similar size. This is partly for visual appeal, but mainly because you want everything to cook at the same speed.

If you are cooking different vegetables together and you know that some cook faster than others, you might want to make those dice a little larger.

Small dice are sometimes called **brunoise** (a French term), and are around 0.5 cm square. This size is good for dicing vegetables to go in dressings and sauces.

Medium dice are usually around 1 cm square, like a playing die. This size is great for dicing vegetables to go in soups and stews.

Large dice are about 2 cm square, which is the perfect size for your vegetables when you're making a robust chicken or beef stock. Stock takes a few hours to make, so you want the vegetables to release their flavours but not disintegrate into the liquid.

Kitchen 101:
Stocking your Pantry

with Alice Zaslavsky

When you first start cooking, the array of ingredients on offer can seem overwhelming. But lots of them get used over and over in different recipes, and most of them keep well in the pantry or fridge (see page 52). So, what are the essentials? What are the go-to ingredients that you can buy now to keep you covered so that you can cook any of your favourites whenever you want? The list below will cover you for a wide range of recipes!

Basics
sea salt flakes
black peppercorns
extra virgin olive oil
vegetable oil
white wine vinegar
balsamic vinegar

Baking needs
plain flour
self-raising flour
bicarbonate of soda
　(baking soda)
baking powder
caster sugar

Rice and grains
jasmine rice
Arborio rice
dried spaghetti
dried penne

Cans
cannellini beans
chickpeas
whole tomatoes
tomato paste
tuna in oil
anchovy fillets
coconut cream
coconut milk

Dried herbs and spices
chilli powder/flakes
smoked paprika
ground cinnamon
ground cumin
ground coriander
ground turmeric
bay leaves
dried oregano
dried rosemary
dried thyme

Pickled vegetables
olives
capers
gherkins

Miscellaneous
jam
Vegemite
honey
whole-egg mayonnaise
Dijon or wholegrain
　mustard
tomato sauce
soy sauce
fish sauce
sesame oil
chicken stock
curry paste
curry powder
panko breadcrumbs

Kitchen 101:
Chicken

with Jake Smyth

Chicken is Australians' favourite meat — we eat an average of 46 kg of chicken per person per year, putting Australia in the top 10 chicken-eating countries in the world! But do you know what to look for when buying chicken? What's the difference between free-range and organic? What are the different cuts of chicken and what do you use them for? And how — and for how long — can you store raw and cooked chicken?

How can I tell if chicken is fresh?

Colour

The colour of the chicken can vary depending on the breed, what it's been fed and on the age of the chicken at slaughter. In general, the meat should be a light pink, with no discolouration or greyness. Some dark red spots are normal — these are caused during the butchering process, by burst blood vessels or marrow from broken bones leaching into the meat.

Touch

Chicken can feel wet, but should not feel slimy. Sliminess on chicken meat is caused by bacteria creating a biofilm and is a sign that the chicken is beginning to spoil. If you are confident that the chicken has been stored properly, and it still smells and looks fresh, it is still OK to consume if you give it a good wash and cook it thoroughly. If in any doubt, throw it out.

Smell

If it stinks, it's probably off. Fresh chicken should have no strong aroma — a sour, rancid smell is a surefire way to tell that the chicken is no longer safe to eat.

What's the difference between free-range and organic?

Free-range chickens are allowed to run free during the day and are kept in sheds at night to protect them from predators and extreme weather conditions. The stocking density for free-range chickens is capped at 10,000 hens per hectare.

Organic chickens are fed organic produce that has no pesticides or chemicals added. An organic chicken is not necessarily also free-range.

What's the difference between light meat and dark meat?

Dark meat refers to the muscles in the chicken that do more work (thighs, drumsticks) and are therefore darker in colour due to myoglobin (this is a protein that stores oxygen in the muscles). Light meat refers to the muscles that do less work (breasts, tenderloins) and are therefore lighter in colour.

Dark meat responds well to long cooking times, as it has more fat and connective tissue — these break down slowly and keep the meat moist over a longer exposure to heat. Light meat responds better to quicker and more intense cooking, as the lack of fat can cause it to dry out.

How much chicken makes a single portion?

A single portion of meat is considered to weigh 150–200 g. An average (single) chicken breast in Australia weighs 300 g.

Should I cook with the skin on or off?

This is usually a matter of personal and health preference. Most pre-packaged chicken is sold without skin, but cooking with the skin on can keep moisture and flavour in the meat. (Also, skin is crazy delicious — chicken crackling, anyone?)

How can I tell if my chicken is cooked?

The easiest way to tell if chicken is cooked is by the colour — the meat turns white as it cooks. Otherwise, as a rule of thumb, light meat should be cooked to an internal temperature of 62°C and dark meat to 74°C. Measure with a meat thermometer pushed into the thickest part of the chicken. Alternatively, make a small cut through to the middle of the chicken and lightly press on the surface with the flat of the knife — the juices emerging should run out clear. Make another cut between the thigh and the breast and check the juices again.

How should chicken be stored?

Raw

Raw chicken should be stored in the wrapping it was purchased in or in an airtight container in the fridge (1°C–5°C) for no longer than 3 days. Keep the meat as dry as possible (i.e. the chicken should not be sitting in a pool of water) by giving it a light pat with paper towels before storing. The container should be labelled with the date and kept on the lowest shelf of the fridge to prevent cross-contamination should the container leak.

Cooked

Cooked chicken should also be stored in an airtight container in the fridge and be consumed within 3 days. Make sure that the chicken has cooled before storing it — this prevents the temperature of the fridge from fluctuating too much — and store it clearly labelled.

Is it OK to freeze chicken?

Both raw and cooked chicken can be frozen safely. It's best to consume either within a month, and in the case of cooked chicken, make sure that it's thoroughly reheated before eating. To prevent freezer burn (caused by exposure to air in the freezer), make sure every surface of the chicken is covered. Plastic wrap is a great tool, as are ziplock bags with the air pushed out.

Refreezing either raw or cooked chicken after thawing is not advised, so to avoid food waste, cut the chicken into portions before freezing it.

Thawing should be done in the fridge, overnight. Place the chicken container/bag in a deep tray on the lowest shelf, to prevent contamination of other items should there be leakage.

What are the main cuts of chicken?

Breast
Generally the largest muscle on the bird, the breast meat usually includes the tenderloin. Breast meat can sometimes be sold as a double (forming a large heart-shape). The meat is generally quite lean, and a favourite among fitness fanatics for its high protein-to-fat ratio. It's usually sold with the skin off.

Tenderloin
The tenderloin is a strip of meat that lies beneath the bulk of the breast meat on the chicken's sternum. It is considered a more tender cut than the breast, as it's the part of the muscle that does the least work. It's commonly used in stir-fries and chicken fingers.

Maryland
This is basically the leg of the chicken. It consists of both the thigh and the drumstick, and is usually sold with the bone in and the skin on. Marylands sometimes include the oyster, which is a small oval of flesh near the spine and attached to the top of the thigh.

Wing
The wing can be split into three main sections: the drummette, the mid-wing (or mid-joint) and the wing tip. The drummette and the mid-wing are the most popular cuts for easy finger food, and the tips are very useful for adding flavour to stocks.

Thigh
The upper part of the leg of the chicken, thigh meat is slightly darker than breast meat, as the thigh is a muscle that does more work. Thighs are usually sold either as cutlets (with bone in and skin on) or as fillets (boneless and skinless).

Drumstick
The drumstick is the lower part of the leg. Think of it as the calves of the chicken. It's usually also sold with the bone in and the skin on.

CHECK OUT NATHAN SASI'S ROAST CHICKEN WITH REAL GRAVY RECIPE ON PAGE 162.

Kitchen 101:
Fish

with Josh Niland

If you're cooking with fish, the most important thing is freshness. But how can you tell if fish is fresh? And how long can you safely keep it for? Here are the basics on cooking with fish.

What should I look for?

Smell
Fresh fish shouldn't smell 'fishy'. It should have a faint smell of seawater, if it smells at all. Some people liken the smell of fresh fish to that of fresh milk.

Colour
As fish ages, its colour starts to dull, so look for specimens with good colour. Fresh salmon and other red fish should still have a lovely vibrant colour and should not be turning brown. White fish should look bright and white, not washed out.

Texture
The flesh should be firm and intact, with no signs of bruising or damaging, and should bounce back when pressed gently. The proteins in fish start to degrade over time, so fish that's not fresh will start to feel soft and mushy. Fish with the skin on should have a slightly slimy texture on the skin.

Bonus points for whole fish
Whole fish should be in good condition, with spotting and colouring retained and fins intact. The eyes should be rounded and pronounced, and clear rather than cloudy. Look for red gills that are dry to the touch.

What if it's packaged up and I can't get a close look at it?

Check the use-by dates on the packaging, and avoid any packaging that shows condensation. In the supermarket it's a good idea to stick to popular species like ocean trout and barramundi — they have the highest sales turnover, so are more likely to be fresh.

How long will fish keep for?

It's best to cook fresh fish on the same day you buy it, but if that's not possible use it within 1–2 days of purchasing. Store the fish in the coldest part of your fridge, wrapped in plastic wrap and then paper (or in a sealed container).

Fish can also be frozen for up to 3 months. Pat the fish dry, place it in an airtight freezer bag and extract as much air as possible before freezing.

Once cooked, fish will last for 2–3 days in the fridge or 3–4 months in the freezer. Place the cooked fish in a shallow airtight container, or wrap it tightly in aluminium foil or plastic wrap. Refrigerate or freeze within 2 hours of cooking.

What's the story with different cuts of fish?

Cutlet

A cutlet is a piece cut from across the fish, typically with the backbone still in and the skin still on. Cutlets are often called 'steaks'. They take longer to cook, but are more flavoursome.

Fillet

A fillet is cut from the side of fish and is usually boneless. Fillets may be sold with the skin on or off. They are the easiest and fastest cuts to cook.

Side

A side of fish is a piece cut along the central skeleton of the fish from spine to belly. A side of fish may still contain small pin bones throughout.

Whole

A whole fish is intact from head to tail. Whole fish sold for domestic use are often gutted and scaled, giving the home cook an easier time. Cooking with whole fish can be quite economical.

What's the difference between farmed and wild-caught fish?

Farmed fish are bred in an enclosed and semi-controlled environment. The fish are fed consistently and protected from natural predators. The confinement controls the size of the fish and allows the farmers to produce a consistent product. This is generally considered to be more sustainable than wild fishing, but not all breeds of fish and seafood can be successfully farmed.

Wild-caught fish are highly seasonal and can vary greatly in size and number depending on the fishing conditions that day. Some wild-caught fish are under threat of overfishing, and the practice is controversial in certain parts of the world. However, there are still some popular breeds of fish that are not farm-friendly — large species of tuna favoured by the Japanese, for example, cannot viably be bred in a farm.

Kitchen 101:
Beef

with Alice Zaslavsky

When it comes to beef, there are so many different cuts to choose from. What's the difference between a primary cut and a secondary cut? Is eye fillet the same as scotch fillet? Here we take you through the basics so you'll know what you're looking for when you visit the supermarket or the butcher. Regardless of which cut you choose, look for a bright red, vivid colour to the meat and a creamy-white colour to the fat.

What are primary and secondary cuts?

The cut of meat you are using will define how you should cook it for the best results. Here's the rundown on primary and secondary cuts.

Primary cuts
These cuts of meat are prized for their tenderness. The muscles in these cuts tend not to do as much work as the ones that make up the secondary cuts, and take well to fast cooking methods like pan-frying. They are also the kinds of cuts that you would eat medium-rare, as they tend to toughen and dry out considerably if overcooked.

Secondary cuts
These cuts of meat are from the muscles that do the most work in the animal. Because of this, the muscles tend to have a lot of intramuscular fat and collagen. These break down with low-and-slow cooking methods. Secondary cuts tend to have the most flavour and are best used in slow roasts, casseroles, stews and curries.

What are the basic primary cuts?

Eye fillet
Also known as tenderloin, this cut of meat comes from a tapered strip in the centre of the cow's back. The meat is very lean and tender. It is the cut used to make steak tartare, as it has a very low amount of gristle through the meat.

Scotch fillet
Also known as rib eye, this cut of steak comes from the middle of the cow, right next to the rib, and usually has a good amount of intramuscular fat, making it a tender cut to eat.

Sirlion
The sirloin is cut from the back of the cow. It is a cheaper cut than eye or scotch fillet, but is still good for pan-frying and barbecuing.

T-bone
The T-bone is cut from the short loin of the cow, and is made up of a T-shaped bone with meat either side.

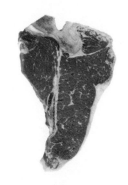

What are the basic secondary cuts?

Rump steak
Unsurprisingly, this comes from the rump of the cow. These steaks are quite lean and not very fatty, which means that cooking high and fast is essential. Rump steak is great in stir-fries.

Chuck steak
Chuck steaks come from the shoulders of the cow, which are tough muscles with some intramuscular fat. This cut works well in curries and stews.

Brisket
These are famously used in Texan barbecues, as the large amount of connective tissues helps keep the meat tender while being smoked. Brisket is also used for making pastrami.

TIP
Get to know your local butcher.

Kitchen 101:
Carving Roasts

with Alice Zaslavsky

Whether it's a roast chicken, a boneless or a bone-in roast, there are some basic steps to mastering carving.

What gear do I need?

Cutting board
You can essentially use any clean cutting board to carve your roast on. There are some specific boards on the market — carving boards can have grooves near the edge to capture leaking juices, and carving platters can have spikes to hold the meat in place — but these are gadgets with just one use, and nobody's got time for that.

Knife
It's best to get a sharp, long, straight-edged knife. Serrated knives tear rather than slice the fibres of the meat, and shorter knives promote sawing rather than slicing, resulting in an inconsistent slice.

Carving fork
A carving fork is a secondary tool — it's really there just to hold the meat in place without burning your fingers. You could use a pair of tongs (if you're feeling dexterous) or a regular fork, but the length of the tines on a carving fork really do help to keep the meat in place while you're wielding the knife.

Do I really need to rest the meat before I start carving?

Yes! It's very important to let the meat rest before carving. The heat from cooking pushes all the juices into the centre of the roast, and resting the meat allows them to be redistributed through the meat fibres, meaning that you're squeezing out less juice onto the board (or your table) as you're carving. It also means that you get evenly moist slices of meat from your roast.

Does it matter which direction I cut in?

Most of the fibres in a piece of muscle run parallel, like lengths of rope laid down beside each other. This is known as 'the grain'. It's advised to carve the meat 'across the grain' — perpendicular to how the fibres run — as this results in a more tender slice due to the natural separation of the fibres.

What's the best way to slice?

To create even slices, try to use a long, fluid motion as much as possible. Think of it as the 'motion of the ocean'. Avoid jagged motions like sawing — this creates little edges on the face of the slice, so it won't be evenly thick. A blunt knife can also lead to sawing, which tears the fibres of the meat rather than slicing through them.

Should I go with bone in or bone out?

Roasts come in many forms and they're all delicious. When it comes to carving, the biggest difference is whether you're dealing with a roast that's got bones or not.

Boneless roasts are the easiest to carve, as you can run a knife straight through the meat without worrying about having obstacles to carve around.

Bone-in roasts have a few different scenarios:
- **Rib roasts** have four to eight bones sticking out in a row from the piece of meat. You usually carve between the bones to separate each lollipop-like serve of roast.
- **Leg roasts** usually have a single large bone running through the centre of the roast. This can make them hard to carve, as you can't slice through the meat in one go. One way to carve a leg roast is to slice the meat through to the bone and then run your knife close along the bone to cut the slices off.
- **Shoulder roasts** with the bone in are the hardest to carve. This is because the shoulder blade isn't a consistent size or shape, and the muscle fibres run in groups, in different directions. Recipes for shoulder meat often call for long and slow cooking methods, because the shoulder is a tougher cut of meat. Slower cooking methods result in a tender, pull-apart texture that you can easily remove in chunks.

What about carving poultry?

The easiest way to carve poultry is to break down the whole bird into legs, thighs, wings and breasts. That way you get complete serves and you don't have to worry about slicing through to bones that refuse to lie flat. When approaching the task, think about how the bird moves, and look for the natural breaks. Starting with the spot where the leg moves away from the breast, hold the knife as close to the breast as possible and slice through. Turn the bird over and use the knife to help remove the thigh from the chicken frame. Repeat for the other thigh and the wings. Flip the bird back over, place your knife between the breast bone and the breast and gently encourage each breast to come off the frame.

If you want to carve slices from your poultry — and this makes a bit more sense for large birds, like turkey — remove each cut of meat (e.g. the breast) from the bone and then slice it into boneless pieces.

Kitchen 101:
Fruit & Veg

with Analiese Gregory

When it comes to fruit and veg, the best tip is to buy what's in season. Not only will it taste better, but it'll be easier on your pocket too. At the height of each season, different fruit and veg are plentiful and at their peak, which drives prices down and means you get to enjoy better quality on a smaller budget. Look out for the specials, which can be a good guide to what's in season.

What are the signs to look for in fresh fruit and veg?

To pick out the freshest fruit and veg, you have to use your senses. Don't be afraid to handle the fruit and veg while you're in the store — you won't be able to sort the gems from the duds unless you do. Pick it up, look at it, feel it and smell it.

Here are our tips on some of Australia's favourite fruit and veg:

Apples and pears should be firm, with no bruises. Don't worry about the shine — it doesn't mean much, as farmers often wax their fruit before it goes on sale.

Asparagus should be bright green, with firm, closed tips. Avoid tips that are open and spreading, which is a sign of age.

Avocados grow hanging from a tree, so watch out for flat or black spots — these

tell you that the avo has been dropped or damaged. Avocados soften as they ripen, so you should buy a firm avocado, especially if you're not eating it immediately.

Broccoli is best when the stalks are firm with crisp leaves, and the florets are dark green. If the leaves or the buds are yellow in colour, move on.

Carrots should be firm, plump and smooth, with no cracks.

Cauliflower should be creamy white in colour, and ideally the head will be protected with lots of thick green leaves. Avoid caulis that are spotted or dull, or have small flowers appearing.

Cherries with the stems intact will last longer. Choose cherries that are plump and darker in colour (although some varieties are naturally pale).

Citrus fruit should be firm but slightly springy, and lightly fragrant. Choose specimens that are heavy for their size, and avoid any that are shrivelled.

Eggplants should have firm, smooth skin that bounces back when pressed. Avoid eggplants that sound hollow when tapped lightly with your knuckles — this indicates dryness.

Garlic bulbs typically contain 10 to 20 individual cloves. Choose bulbs that are firm and plump rather than soft or spongy. The papery outer skin of the bulb should be intact.

Grapes should be firmly attached to their stems, with no spots or wrinkles.

Green beans are best when crisp, slender and bright in colour, with no blemishes.

Lettuce and other leafy greens should be crisp rather than limp. As you'll be discarding several of the outer leaves, look inside and check that the inner leaves look healthy and are relatively unmarked.

Melons grow on a vine on the ground, so flat spots are okay. Look for a melon that is heavy for its size and smells fragrant. Ripe melons smell much more strongly than unripe ones.

Onions should be odourless — any smell is a sign of bruising under the skin. Look for onions that are heavy for their size with dry skins. Avoid onions that are sprouting.

Pineapples should smell sweet at the stem end. The leaves should look fresh, not brown or dry.

Potatoes and other root vegetables are seasonal, believe it or not. In Australia, the potato season begins in November/ December. Pick firm potatoes that aren't sprouting or green in colour — once a potato begins to sprout new life, it's no longer suitable for eating. Avoid root vegetables with cracks on the base, which indicates dryness.

Pumpkins should be firm and produce a solid, woody sound when firmly tapped with your knuckles. Avoid any with discoloured, bruised or cracked skin.

Strawberries are best when evenly red in colour, without any yellow or green. Always check the bottom of the container for hidden spoiled fruit.

Tomatoes should be firm but with a little give. The smell is important — the stem end should retain a sweet, woody aroma. Wrinkles on tomatoes are a sign of age.

What about herbs?

As with any leafy veg, look for herbs that are bright and full of life, as opposed to dark and limp. The key to storing herbs is keeping them moist. You can put your herbs in a cup of water — just like a bunch of flowers — and keep them in the fridge. You can also place your herbs between lightly dampened paper towels and store them in a ziplock bag in the fridge.

A good trick for preserving the life of herbs is to make them into herb oils — this works well with basil and similar herbs. Blitz the herb in a blender with a little olive oil, then pour the mixture into ice-cube trays and store them in the freezer. When you're ready to use the herb oils, pop the cubes out of the tray and drop them into the frying pan, or throw them into your pasta and mix through.

Kitchen 101:
Rice

with Alice Zaslavsky

Many new cooks struggle to cook rice, either burning it or undercooking it for fear of burning it! Or they put much too much water in and the rice doesn't fluff up nicely. Now you never have to burn rice again — cooking it is easy if you follow our steps.

How much rice should I cook?

One cup of raw rice will yield 2–3 cups of cooked rice, which is plenty for two servings as an accompaniment to a main meal.

Don't let cooked rice sit around at room temperature, as it can grow bacteria quickly. If you have leftover rice, place it in a container with an airtight lid and store it in the fridge for 3–4 days or the freezer for up to 3 months.

What are the basic steps to cooking rice?

1   Rinse your rice to remove excess starch. Put it in a medium-sized bowl and cover it with cold water. Stir it around a bit with your hands — the water will turn cloudy — then tip everything into a large sieve to drain off the water. You can repeat the rinsing if you wish to get rid of even more starch.

2   Tip the well-drained rice into a saucepan that has a tight-fitting lid, and pour in enough water to cover the rice by 2.5 cm (you'll soon learn to judge this accurately — some people use a knuckle). Bring the water to the boil, while stirring, and hold it at a light boil for 5 minutes. Place a piece of aluminium foil over the saucepan before putting on the lid, then turn the heat off. **Do not lift the lid** for at least 15 minutes — the steam in the saucepan is essential for a great result.

3   When done, use a fork to fluff up the rice. This releases the steam so that your rice does not overcook.

If you're serving the rice with a curry or something similar, there is no need to add salt. For a tasty variation, make coconut rice by adding a slice of ginger and replacing some of the water with coconut cream before boiling it.

What sort of rice should I use?

There are over 40,000 varieties of rice around the world! They are often classified by the size and/or shape of the grain and how sticky they are. Colour also comes into the equation, with white and brown rice being the most popular. In Australia, the six most common varieties of rice are as follows.

Long-grain has long, slim grains that tend to remain separate. This rice is often steamed and served as an accompaniment to a savoury meal.

Medium-grain has shorter, fatter grains than long-grain, and the cooked grains tend to stick together. It is used in sushi and some puddings.

Short-grain has short grains that stick together when cooked, and is typically used in puddings.

Basmati is a type of long-grain rice with very slim, long grains and a good flavour, and is frequently used in Indian cooking.

Arborio is a short-grain rice that is particularly suited to cooking risottos.

Jasmine is a long-grain, slightly perfumed rice that is slightly more sticky than other long-grain rices, and is often used in Thai cooking.

TIP
Brown rice is widely considered to be a healthier choice than white, because it's a whole grain (all parts of the grain have been retained). White rice has had some of the nutritious parts of the grain removed.

If you could only pick one type of rice to cook with for all occasions, one of the best choices is jasmine rice. It's a beautiful fragrant rice that's reliable and cooks quickly, and it can be used in sweet and savoury dishes. Note, though, that if you want to cook a risotto, you must use Arborio rice (or another type of risotto rice). The high starch content in Arborio rice enables it to hold eight times its weight in moisture, giving you a creamy risotto with plump grains that won't fall apart.

Kitchen 101:
Pasta

with Alice Zaslavsky

You'll probably find yourself cooking with pasta quite often — it is a marvellously versatile ingredient. You can whip up a sauce and serve it over fettuccine for a quick evening meal, have friends round to share a massive lasagne, or pop some pasta in a Mediterranean-style salad to take on a picnic. The Italians, who brought us pasta, invented over 300 different shapes to suit almost any type of meal. So, here's a guide on what to buy and how to use it.

Why is some pasta so much more expensive?

Prices for pasta can range from less than $1 to $15 for 500 g. It all depends on the quality, which in turn depends on the ingredients and how it is made. Buy the best quality you can afford — it's a lot easier to overcook cheap pasta.

The best dried pasta is made with durum wheat (hard flour) and water. Cheaper pasta has other ingredients in it, including ordinary wheat flour. When buying pasta, look for '100% durum wheat flour' on the packet. Australia produces excellent pasta due to the great durum wheat we grow. Good-quality dried pasta will also have a slightly rough surface to help the sauce stick to it.

Fresh pasta is sometimes egg-based and may be made with a softer wheat flour.

Why all the different shapes?

Each type of pasta shape works best with a certain type of meal.
- Soups (such as minestrone) and salads suits smaller shapes, twists and circles. **Risoni**, which is a rice-shaped pasta, is great in these.
- Rich, chunky sauces, such as Bolognese, are best with thick ribbons such as **pappardelle** or **lasagne**, or ribbed, angular or tubular pastas such as **penne**.
- Lighter, smoother sauces, such as pesto, suit twists like **fusilli**, as the sauce will cling to the twists.
- Baked cheese dishes are best with tubular pastas like **penne** or **macaroni**.
- Creamy sauces, such as carbonara, or simple oil and herb dressings suit long, skinny strands like **spaghetti**, **fettuccine** or **linguine**.

But if you only have spaghetti on hand, then use spaghetti!

How much do I need?

As a rough guide, 500 g of dried pasta feeds 4-6 people. When measuring out your pasta, allow about:
- 100 g dried pasta per person
- 150 g fresh pasta per person.

How do I cook it just right?

It's best to use a large, heavy-based pot.

To the pot, add 1 litre of water for every 100 g of pasta you are going to cook. Then add an extra 1 litre 'for the pot'. So, for 500 g of pasta you will need 6 litres of water.

Put the pot on the cooktop, cover it with a lid and bring it to the boil. Remove the lid and keep heating until you have a rolling boil — large bubbles coming up all over your pot that won't go away if you stir the water.

Now add salt — as a general rule, 1 tablespoon of salt for every 2 litres of water. Your 500 g of pasta will need 3 tablespoons of salt. It sounds like a lot, but if you don't season the water your pasta will taste flabby and flat. Most of it gets tipped out with the cooking water, but you do need a decent amount in there to start with so that it can get absorbed into the pasta.

Next, add the pasta. Just tip smaller shapes in. With long strands, hold all the pasta in a bunch vertically, just above the water, and drop it in. Once the bottom ends have softened (this only takes a couple of minutes), use a fork to gently stir until all of the pasta is in the water.

You might find that the pot goes off the boil temporarily when you add the pasta. Bring it back up to the boil (with the lid off) and boil until done. The length of time stated on the packet will guide you. Depending on the size, shape and thickness of the pasta:
- fresh pasta typically cooks in 2-3 minutes
- dried pasta typically cooks in 5-12 minutes.

It will be ready when the pasta is still firm but has no chalky centre — use a wooden spoon to lift a piece out and cut it open. If it is still chalky, keep cooking for another minute, then check again. Overcooking the pasta will result in a sticky, flabby mess.

When it's ready, drain the pasta in a colander and serve it straight away.

What does 'al dente' mean?

Pasta cooking instructions often say cook until 'al dente'. This translates as 'to the tooth', and means that it will be firm, but not crunchy, when you bite down on it. Always check the texture of your pasta before serving it.

More pasta tips

- Never rinse pasta (unless you're cooking with fresh lasagne sheets) — you want the starch to stay on the pasta so that the sauce sticks to it.
- Likewise, don't add oil to the pasta water, or the sauce won't stick.
- Save a cup of pasta cooking water to thin down your sauce if required.
- Have the sauce or ingredients ready for when the pasta is done, and have your serving bowls ready warmed.
- Use a good-quality hard cheese for serving, i.e. Parmesan or Pecorino. As a general rule, don't serve cheese with a fish-based pasta sauce.
- For magazine-looking spaghetti, use tongs to twist the spaghetti in the bowl of a ladle, then carefully transfer it into a warmed, shallow bowl.

FUSILLI

FETTUCINE

SPAGHETTI (FRESH)

LASAGNE

MACARONI

TORTELLINI

SPAGHETTI (DRIED)

FARFALLE

PENNE

RAVIOLI

CONCHIGLIE (SEASHELL)

RIGATONI

GEMELLI

Kitchen 101:
Oils & Vinegars

with Alice Zaslavsky

Oil and vinegar are two of those basic ingredients that you probably never think about until you start to cook. And then you discover just how many different types there are of each! There are vegetable oils, olive oils, virgin oils, extra virgin oils, coconut oils . . . and butter (although this is a fat rather than an oil, you can cook with it in a similar way). Then there are the vinegars . . . how on earth do you choose which ones to use?

What am I looking for when choosing an oil?

This will depend on whether you're cooking with it or using it for flavour — or both! The quality of the oil along with how it's produced will affect its qualities. The cheaper vegetable oils have generally undergone a number of extraction and refining processes to obtain a clear, stable product. Virgin oils are extracted by pressing only, and are not refined. They tend to have more flavour, but do not keep quite as well as refined oils. Extra virgin oils are similar but are higher in quality and have a better taste.

What does smoke point mean?

When you heat any oil or fat, it gets to a certain temperature where the chemical structure starts breaking down and smoke is produced — this is the smoke point, and it's different for each oil.

Butter, unrefined coconut oil and **extra virgin olive oil** have the lowest smoke points (160-175°C). They each have a particular flavour, which will alter the taste of what's being cooked.

Common oils with a neutral flavour that can handle higher heat (205-240°C) are **canola, vegetable, sunflower** and **blended (non-virgin) olive oil**. These oils are better for deep-frying.

Peanut oil, rice bran oil and **safflower oil** are good choices for stir-frying, as they can handle super-high heat.

What's with all the different olive oils?

Olive oil flavours can be as complex as wines — they vary from mild and fruity to heavy, robust and peppery. It all depends on where they are grown, the climate, when they were picked and what variety the olives are, along with the degree of processing (less is better) and any refining. Generally speaking, the darker the colour, the more full the flavour. Australia is now producing some great olive oils.

Extra virgin olive oil is the king — it's the best in flavour, colour and aroma, and the most expensive of all the olive oils. As such, it's better suited to flavouring dishes rather than for cooking.

Virgin olive oil is the next level down. It is still good, but has less flavour and more acidity than extra virgin.

Refined olive oil is virgin oil that has been refined to remove colour, odour and flavour.

Blended olive oil is a mixture of virgin and refined oils, and will often be labelled 'pure olive oil' or 'extra light olive oil'. It is lighter in flavour but has a higher smoke point than virgin oils. Although it is of a lesser quality, it's a good oil to use for deep-frying.

Which oils are best for cooking and which for dressings?

Blended olive oil is a great all-rounder — excellent for deep-frying, shallow-frying, sautéing and grilling, and due to its mild flavour it's great for a mayonnaise or aïoli.

Extra virgin olive oil is great for giving a final flourish to a dish — drizzle it over soup, risotto, pasta or salad. It's also great as a butter alternative to serve with bread at the dinner table, and is essential to making a beautiful vinaigrette.

Nut oils, **avocado oil** and **sesame oil** are all strongly flavoured, so a little added to a salad dressing can make a big taste difference.

Butter has great flavour, but tends to burn very quickly when you're frying with it. Try adding some light-flavoured olive oil to the butter — this will give you the butter flavour without getting burnt milk solids.

Coconut oils vary in flavour depending on the extraction method used to make them. Use coconut oil in any dish where you will be adding coconut milk or cream. Coconut oil may be solid at room temperature (except at the height of summer!), so you may need to melt it for some uses.

How do I store my oils?

Oils and butter go rancid quickly. Oils that you only use in small amounts should be bought in small quantities, especially nut oils and avocado oil — keep these in the fridge after opening. Olive and other oils should be stored in a cool, dark place away from direct sunlight. Make sure you use them within a few months, as unlike wine (and vinegar) they don't get better with age.

If I can only buy one oil and one vinegar, which ones should I choose?

Extra virgin olive oil all the way, the best quality you can afford. And for vinegar, a good-quality balsamic.

What's so great about balsamic vinegar?

True balsamic vinegar (labelled 'Aceto Balsamico Tradizionale' or 'traditional balsamic vinegar') has been made in Modena, Italy, for over 1,000 years, from the juice (must) of late-harvest Trebbiano grapes. The juice is boiled long and slow, until 30–70 per cent of the liquid has evaporated off and the sugars have caramelised. The cooked product must then undergo a double fermentation process before being aged in barrels for at least 12 years. It is very expensive.

More affordable balsamic vinegars (labelled 'Aceto Balsamico di Modena' or 'Balsamic Vinegar of Modena') are mass-produced and widely available. They are made from wine vinegar with added caramel for colour and sweetness. To be called 'aged', a vinegar must be aged for three years.

True balsamic is used mostly as a condiment — drizzled over a ripe tomato or avocado, it is a thing of beauty. The cheaper version is most often used in salad dressings.

What about other vinegars?

The range of vinegars is vast, and your choice may come down to personal preference. Apple cider vinegar is a healthy option and adds a fruity touch to dressings, while red wine and white wine vinegars are popular in Italian and French cooking. If you are just looking for something to add a little zing to a dressing, you don't need to buy a whole bunch of fancy vinegars — a squeeze of lemon will do the trick.

Kitchen 101:
Keeping Food Fresh

with Alice Zaslavsky

To avoid wasting money by throwing out food that is past it, try to use as much as possible while it is still fresh. You can store the rest following the guidelines below.

How long will my food stay fresh?

Generally, foods will last longer in the fridge than at room temperature, and longer again in the freezer. This is because the bacteria that cause food to spoil don't grow as quickly at colder temperatures. However, some foods are better stored at room temperature than the fridge, and not all foods should be frozen.

At room temperature
Root vegetables (e.g. potatoes, parsnips, carrots, onions) and **pumpkins** stored in a cool, dark cupboard will keep for a week or more. Take them out of any plastic bags to allow them to breathe, and ideally store them in a vegetable rack to let the air circulate underneath. Once they've been cut it's better to store them in the fridge — but don't put potatoes in there.

Many **fruits** (but not berries) will keep in a bowl on the benchtop for a week or more — this includes tomatoes, as their skins can get tough if stored in the fridge. Fruits that are threatening to become overripe can be moved to the fridge for an extra couple of days, but not bananas as they go black very quickly.

For best results with **avocados**, buy them when they're hard and green and let them ripen in your fruit bowl, then transfer them to the fridge as soon as they are nicely ripe.

In the fridge
Buy the largest fridge you can afford, because this is where you'll store a lot of things. Except for whole fruits and vegetables, everything should be wrapped well or stored in a strong container with a well-fitting lid. Your fridge temperature should be no more than 5°C in the main part of the fridge, and you should store raw food below cooked food so that drips from the raw food won't cause contamination.

A rule of thumb is that most foods will keep for about a week, but like everything else there are exceptions. Always check food when you take it out of the fridge — if you think it might be off (see opposite), throw it away immediately. Also throw out anything that's past its use-by date.

Raw fish is best used on the same day, but will keep in the fridge for 1–2 days. Store it at the bottom of the fridge, wrapped in plastic and then paper (or in a sealed container).

Raw chicken and meat will keep for a couple of days. Larger pieces will keep better than smaller ones — minced meat can go off quite quickly. Store meat in sealed containers at the bottom of the fridge.

Dairy products are often stored in compartments in the door. Milk and yoghurt will last up to a week, while cheese will often keep for longer. Make sure the cheese is well wrapped so that it doesn't dry out.

Opened bottles and jars of sauces, jams and other condiments will keep for several weeks if well sealed.

Eggs are best kept in the main part of the fridge, in the cardboard box they came in, to prevent them picking up smells from other foods. They will keep for several weeks.

Leafy and salad vegetables are best stored in the chiller drawer at the bottom of the fridge — most should keep for about a week. Clean the drawer out regularly, as forgotten bits of veg will start going nasty in the corners. Bags of cut salad greens should be plumped up as much as possible and will only keep for a few days at most.

Delicate fruits like berries keep for a day or two, but are best eaten soon after buying.

Any **cut vegetables and fruit** are best in the fridge — either well wrapped in the chiller drawer or in airtight containers in the main part of the fridge. Cut onions are particularly good at transferring their flavour to things like milk and yoghurt, so make sure they are very well wrapped. Use cut vegetables and fruit up within a couple of days, or put them in the freezer instead.

In the freezer

A freezer or fridge-freezer will let you store food for much longer, and can also be used for leftovers (see page 54). The freezer temperature should be -18°C or lower, and the food should be well wrapped and labelled with the date it went in.

All of the times given below are estimates, so food might not keep quite as long (and definitely shouldn't be stored for longer).

Fatty fish will keep for 3 months, other fish for 6 months, and **seafood** (without crumbs or batter) for up to 1 year.

Poultry portions and whole birds can be frozen for 1 year, and minced poultry 4 months.

Red meat is frozen for different times depending on what it is. Beef steaks and roasts, 1 year; pork roasts and loins, 8 months; lamb and veal pieces, 9 months; hams, 2 months. All minced meats can be frozen for up to 4 months, and bacon and sausages for 1 month.

Fruits (including berries) and **fruit juices** will keep for 1 year; **vegetables** for 8 months.

It's best to eat **ice cream** within 2 months, but **butter** will last for 9 months and **cheese** for 3 months. You can freeze **milk** for up to 1 month.

You can't freeze whole **eggs**, but the yolks and whites can be separated and stored in airtight containers in the freezer for up to 1 year.

Baked goods (e.g. cakes, biscuits) and raw cookie or bread dough can be frozen for up to 1 month.

How do I tell when food is off?

It's usually easy to tell when food stored at room temperature or in the fridge is off — it will smell strong or a bit nasty, and may be slimy or have mould growing on it. Food from the freezer is trickier, as it often won't look or smell particularly off. Label all food that goes into the freezer with the date it went in, and just chuck it out if it's too old.

If you're not sure whether something is off or not, don't eat it.

What's the best way to thaw food?

Allow frozen food to thaw in the fridge overnight (or longer for whole poultry and large joints of meat), or in the microwave, following the instructions for your particular machine.

Can I thaw something and refreeze it?

No — thawing food to room temperature lets the bacteria start growing again, so if you refreeze it, then the food might already be spoilt. You can, however, thaw some food, cook it and cool it and *then* refreeze it.

If you've had a power cut for more than a few hours, the food in your freezer will have defrosted to a dangerous level. Take everything out and cook what you can into stews, soups, etc. Refreeze these for later and throw everything else away.

Kitchen 101:
Leftovers

with Alice Zaslavsky

Leftovers are a boon when life is busy, and can also save you money — making a big batch of roast vegetables (see page 191) means that the oven is on just once but you can make several meals. You do, however, need to make sure that you stick to best practice with your leftovers.

What are the most important things to remember?

The four key things you need to do are:

Handle your leftovers hygienically.

Cool them quickly.

Store them at the recommended temperatures (fridge below 5°C, freezer below -18°C).

Eat them up within a reasonable time.

FACT
Low temperatures slow down the rate of microbial growth and any chemical changes in the foods.

How long can I keep cooked food in the fridge?

A general rule is 2-3 days in the fridge for cooked fish and 3-4 days in the fridge for cooked meats and poultry. These items need very careful storage — especially minced meat, with its larger surface area. Get to know your fridge, and always keep cooked leftovers in the coldest part but away from raw food.

Use your eyes and nose — if your leftovers look wrong (i.e. have any discolouration or mould) or smell bad, it's best not to eat them. Food poisoning is the pits!

What about the freezer?

How long you can freeze cooked food depends on what it is:
- 3 months for casseroles, stocks, sauces and soups, and pies
- 1 month for cakes, bread and scones.

Don't freeze anything that has already been frozen beforehand. The exception is ice cream, which (if it lasts that long) will keep for up to 2 months.

What should I store leftovers in?

It is best to store leftovers in glass or strong plastic containers with well-fitting lids. Some things freeze well in ziplock bags, for example Bolognese sauce or pesto. Make sure everything is well sealed — if air gets in, your food will get freezer burn (dry, greyish areas on the surface). The longer the food is in the freezer, the more likely it is to get freezer burn, as no container or bag is completely airtight.

Always leave 1 cm of 'head space' (empty space at the top of the container or bag) to allow for expansion during freezing. Try not to leave more than this, or you'll be wasting space in your freezer.

Always write on the container or bag what the item is and the date it went into the freezer.

How soon should I freeze leftovers?

Try to cool leftovers rapidly after cooking. With large amounts, divide the food up into portions among small, shallow containers so that it cools more quickly. This also makes defrosting easier, and you can just pull out one or more portions when you need them.

As soon as the food is cool, seal the container or bag tightly and place it in the fridge. Once it is well chilled, transfer it to the freezer.

How do I reheat leftovers?

It's best to defrost leftovers in the fridge (not on the bench) for 24 hours.

If you want to defrost leftovers quickly and have a microwave, by all means use that — follow the instructions for your machine. If you don't have a microwave, you can immerse watertight packages in cold water to defrost them.

TIP
A general rule is 2–3 days in the fridge for cooked fish and 3–4 days in the fridge for cooked meats and poultry.

The Basics

Mark Best

Perfectly Boiled Eggs

Serves 1
Cook 6 minutes

EQUIPMENT
nail or needle, small saucepan,
cooktop, egg cups, toaster

INGREDIENTS
2 large free-range eggs (55 g each)
1 slice toast bread
butter
salt and freshly ground black pepper

1   Make sure the eggs are at room temperature — either take them out of the fridge early, or run them under a cold tap until they start not to feel cold anymore. Prick each egg with the nail or needle on the fat end to allow any air to escape; this helps stop the egg cracking when you boil it.

2   Choose a small pan and add enough water that it will just cover the eggs.

3   Bring the water to the boil, then turn down to a low simmer. Carefully add the eggs, using a spoon so that they will not hit the bottom of the pan and crack.

4   Cook for exactly 6 minutes, stirring the eggs from time to time to centre the yolk. Remove the eggs with the spoon and place in the egg cups, thin end up.

5   Meanwhile, toast the bread to your liking and spread it with butter. Cut the toast into soldiers (strips) and serve with the eggs, and salt and pepper on the side.

TIP
If you want to boil eggs for another use, simmer the eggs for 8–9 minutes, then remove and place in a bowl of iced water to stop them cooking. Leave for 10 minutes, then peel the eggs.

Mark Best

Silky Scrambled Eggs

Serves 1
Prep 2 minutes
Cook 2–3 minutes

EQUIPMENT
small non-stick frying pan, wooden
spoon or non-scratch heat-proof
spatula, cooktop, toaster

INGREDIENTS
3 large free-range eggs (55 g each)
a pinch of salt
freshly ground white pepper
butter
1 slice toast bread

1   Tap each egg in turn on the benchtop to
    crack the shell, then break it into a bowl.
    Lightly whisk the eggs with a fork,
    adding a pinch of salt and a good grind
    of pepper.

2   Heat a small non-stick frying pan over
    a moderate heat for a minute or so, then
    add a good knob of butter and let it melt.
    Don't allow the butter to brown, or it will
    discolour the eggs.

3   Meanwhile, put the slice of bread in
    the toaster and start it toasting to
    your liking.

4   Pour the egg mixture into the pan and
    let it sit, without stirring, for 20 seconds.
    Then gently stir with the wooden spoon
    or spatula, lifting and folding the
    mixture over from the bottom of the pan.

5   Let it sit for another 10 seconds, then
    stir and fold again.

6   Repeat until the eggs are softly set
    but still slightly runny in places, then
    remove from the heat and leave for a
    few seconds to finish cooking. Butter
    the toast and serve with the scrambled
    eggs straight away.

Mark Best

Light & Fluffy Omelette

Serves 1
Prep 2 minutes
Cook 2 minutes

EQUIPMENT
small non-stick frying pan, wooden
spoon or non-scratch heat-proof
spatula, cooktop

INGREDIENTS
3 large free-range eggs (55 g each)
a pinch of salt
freshly ground white pepper
a knob of butter

1 Tap each egg in turn on the benchtop to
crack the shell, then break it into a bowl.
Lightly whisk the eggs with a fork,
adding a pinch of salt and a good grind
of pepper.

2 Heat a small non-stick frying pan over
a moderate heat for a minute or so, then
add the butter and wait until it just
begins to foam.

3 Add the eggs and use a wooden spoon
to gently drag egg from the outside of the
pan into the middle, repeating to create
a fluffy layer in the middle.

4 Swirl the runny egg around the edge of
the pan, and wait for the egg to start to
set (around 1 minute).

5 Carefully slide half the omelette onto
a plate, then flip the other half over to
create a semicircle. Serve with bacon,
if desired.

TIP
If you want to serve
your omelette with bacon,
start the bacon frying first,
in another non-stick frying
pan. When it is nearly
ready, start cooking
the omelette.

Mark LaBrooy

Avocado & Tomato
with Poached Eggs

Serves 2
Cook 12 minutes

EQUIPMENT
oven, large and deep saucepan,
cooktop, ovenproof frying pan
(or baking tray), baking paper,
large metal serving spoon, toaster,
slotted spoon

INGREDIENTS

Roast tomatoes
2 tomatoes
1 clove garlic
1 sprig of fresh thyme
1 tablespoon olive oil
salt and freshly ground
　black pepper

Tomato salad & avocado
10 cherry tomatoes
a handful of basil leaves
½ red onion
1 tablespoon olive oil

juice of ½ lemon, plus
　extra for drizzling
salt and freshly ground
　black pepper

To serve
1 avocado
vinegar (about 33 ml per
　litre of poaching water,
　or 1 cup to a 7-litre pan)
2 thick slices of bread
4 eggs
salt and freshly ground
　black pepper
a drizzle of olive oil

1　Preheat the oven to 240°C. Fill the large,
deep saucepan with water and bring it
to the boil, then cover and turn the heat
down until the water barely simmers.

2　While the water is heating, slice the
tomatoes in half horizontally. Trim
the bottom off the garlic clove, remove
the skin and chop the garlic into thin
slices and then small pieces. Pick the
leaves from the thyme sprig, discarding
the stalk.

TIP
Very fresh eggs are best
for poaching. The most
common poaching mistakes
are boiling the water too
furiously, stirring the water
too hard, or not using
enough vinegar.

3   Line the ovenproof frying pan (or baking tray) with baking paper. Place the tomatoes, cut-side up, on the baking paper. Top the tomatoes with the garlic slices and thyme, then drizzle with the olive oil and season to taste with salt and pepper. Place the tomatoes in the oven to roast for 10 minutes.

4   While the tomatoes are roasting, slice the cherry tomatoes in half horizontally and place them in a small bowl with the basil leaves. Trim the top off the onion and cut it in half through the root. Remove the dry layers of skin, then slice half the onion into long, fine slivers, discarding the root. Add the onion slivers to the bowl and set the other uncut half aside for another use. Add the oil and lemon juice, toss together gently and set aside.

5   Halve the avocado by slicing down from the narrow end until your knife meets the seed. Follow the natural path of the knife around the avocado seed in one smooth motion until you meet up with your entry point. Separate the two halves gently; one half will still contain the seed.

6   Whack the avocado seed with the heel of your knife so that the blade is wedged into the seed, then gently twist the knife to remove the seed. Use a large metal serving spoon to scoop out the avocado flesh in one large piece from each avocado half.

7   Cut thin slices into each avocado half without cutting all the way through to the base (the narrow end) — the base will hold each piece of avocado together. Push down with your hand so that the slices fan out from the base and look pretty. Squeeze some lemon juice over the avocado to stop it from browning. Season with salt and pepper to taste, and set aside.

8 Remove the lid from the pan of water and bring it back to the boil — above simmering point, but not on a crazy boil. Add the vinegar to the poaching water; this will help the eggs hold together. Don't add any salt to the water, as it will break down the proteins in your eggs and make them run.

9 Place your bread in the toaster while you poach the eggs. Use a large spoon to stir the water in the pan, creating a small vortex (this keeps the eggs from spreading out). Tap each egg in turn on the benchtop to crack the shell, then hold it directly over the water and break it straight into the vortex. Poach the eggs in the gently boiling water for 2 minutes to achieve yolks that are still soft and slightly runny.

10 Use a slotted spoon to carefully remove each egg from the poaching water, and transfer it onto a tray covered with a clean tea towel to drain off excess water. Lightly season the eggs with salt.

11 To assemble the dish, place a slice of toast on each plate and drizzle with olive oil. Arrange the avocado fans and roasted tomatoes on the toast, then top with the poached eggs and dressed salad. Season to taste, and serve immediately.

Giovanni Pilu

Spaghetti Bolognese

Serves 4
Prep 15 minutes
Cook 1 hour, 15 minutes

EQUIPMENT
large deep frying pan (or cooktop-safe casserole pot), wooden spoon, large saucepan, cooktop, colander

INGREDIENTS
1 onion
1 clove garlic
1 small carrot
400 g can of whole peeled tomatoes
2 tablespoons olive oil
250 g pork mince
250 g veal or beef mince
1 tablespoon tomato paste
100 ml (5 tablespoons) red wine
1 cup veal or beef stock
2 bay leaves
salt and freshly ground black pepper
12 g (1 tablespoon) butter
500 g packet dried spaghetti (alternatively, fettuccini or tagliatelle are great)
4 tablespoons grated Parmesan cheese

1 Chop the vegetables:
   - Trim the top off the onion and cut it in half through the root. Remove the dry layers of skin, then cut each onion half into small dice, discarding the root.
   - Trim the bottom off the garlic clove, remove the skin and chop the garlic into thin slices and then small pieces.
   - Peel the carrot, trim off both ends and cut the carrot in half lengthways. Cut each half into three or four long pieces and then into small dice.

2   Tip the canned tomatoes into a bowl and squash them
    with your fingers.

3   Heat the large, deep frying pan (or cooktop-safe casserole
    pot) over a high heat. Add the oil, onion, garlic and carrot
    and cook, stirring, for 2–3 minutes, until the onion has
    softened.

4   Add both types of mince, spreading it over the pan.
    Do not stir for about 5 minutes, until the meat is well
    browned on one side. Then turn the mince over and
    brown the other side, breaking any lumps up with a
    wooden spoon. Add the tomato paste and cook for
    2 minutes, stirring to combine.

5   Add the wine and allow it to evaporate for 30 seconds,
    then pour in the stock and the squashed canned
    tomatoes. Add the bay leaves and stir to combine.

6   Season to taste with salt and freshly ground black pepper.
    Give it a stir, bring to the boil and reduce the heat to low.
    Simmer for 1 hour, or until thickened. If the sauce is
    thickening too quickly, you can add a little more stock
    or water. Once the Bolognese sauce is thickened to your
    liking, stir through the butter to bring the sauce together.

7   When the Bolognese is nearly ready, put a large saucepan
    of salted water on to boil.

8   Cook the pasta in the boiling water according to the
    packet instructions until al dente (just firm to the bite).
    Dip out a cup of the cooking water, then drain the pasta
    in a colander and return it to the pan.

9   Toss approximately half of the sauce through the
    spaghetti, adding a little of the pasta cooking water if it
    looks too thick. Divide it between the serving bowls and
    top with extra Bolognese and the grated Parmesan.

Monday Morning Cooking Club

Hearty, Healthy Chicken Soup

Makes 3–4 litres
(12–16 cups)
Prep 20 minutes
Cook 1½–2 hours
+ 30 minutes cooling
+ overnight chilling

EQUIPMENT
paper towels, large stockpot with lid,
cooktop, large sieve, large bowl

INGREDIENTS
1 whole chicken
2 kg chicken frames
1 large onion
2 medium carrots
2-3 stems of dill
salt and freshly ground black pepper

This traditional Jewish recipe for chicken soup comes from the Monday Morning Cooking Club's recent book *The Feast Goes On*. The recipe belongs to Lena at the Balaclava Deli in Melbourne.

Lena says:
This is the soup sold at the deli. It is made with lots of chicken bones, creating a clear, rich soup that jellies when cold. It is best served piping hot with noodles, sliced carrot and shredded chicken meat.

1   Start this recipe the day before serving. Prepare the ingredients:
    · Wash the chicken and the chicken frames under cold running water, and pat dry with paper towels. Cut the legs and wings off the chicken, through the joints, then cut the carcass into four pieces.
    · Leaving the onion unpeeled, cut it into quarters through the root. Peel the carrots.

2 Put all the ingredients except the salt and pepper in the large stockpot. Pour in enough cold water to just cover — you will need around 3-4 litres (12-16 cups).

3 Bring to the boil. Skim off the scum that rises to the surface, then cover with the lid on a slight angle, and continue to cook at a light boil for 1½-2 hours.

4 Allow to cool for 30 minutes before removing the bones and straining the soup into the large bowl, discarding everything except the carrots. Add salt and pepper to taste. Allow to cool fully, then refrigerate overnight.

5 The next day, cut the carrots in half lengthways and then chop them into bite-sized pieces. Skim off the fat from the top of the soup, leaving the clear jelly behind. Add the carrot to the soup and reheat it over a moderate heat, tasting for seasoning and flavour. If the flavour is not strong enough, bring to the boil and reduce at a light boil to reach the desired taste; if the flavour is too strong, add some water.

6 Serve within 3 days (store in the fridge), or freeze for future use. Defrost and reheat to serve.

Martin Boetz

Three Easy
Salad Dressings

Prep 2 minutes

EQUIPMENT
graduated measuring cup, jar with
lid, fine-holed grater

METHOD
The rough rule of thumb with salad dressing is 1 part
vinegar/acid to 2 parts oil, plus any flavourings. Once you
know this principle, get creative with what you have hanging
around at home, or follow your own flavour preferences.

French Vinaigrette
(makes about 220 ml)
1 shallot
50 ml white wine vinegar
150 ml olive oil
1 tablespoon Dijon mustard
a pinch of sugar
salt flakes
freshly ground black pepper

1   Trim the top off the shallot and cut it in half through
    the root. Remove the dry layers of skin, then slice each
    shallot half into small dice, discarding the root.

2   Place all the ingredients in a jar. Shake to combine, then
    pour dressing over your favourite salad ingredients just
    before serving.

Light & Creamy Yoghurt Dressing

(makes about ½ cup)
25 ml apple cider vinegar
60 ml olive oil
2 tablespoons plain yoghurt
juice of ¼ lemon
salt flakes
freshly ground black pepper
a pinch of sugar

1   Place all the ingredients in a jar.
    Shake to combine, then pour
    dressing over your favourite salad
    ingredients just before serving.

Soy, Honey & Ginger Dressing

(makes about 200 ml)
1 shallot
1 thumb-sized piece ginger
30 ml (1½ tablespoons) light soy sauce
20 ml (1 tablespoon) white vinegar
100 ml (5 tablespoons) olive oil
1 tablespoon liquid honey
freshly ground black pepper

1   Trim the top off the shallot. Remove the dry layers of skin, then discard the root. Grate the shallot, measuring out about 1 tablespoon. Place the grated shallot in a jar.

2   Peel the ginger, then grate it on the fine-holed grater. Add it to the jar with the remaining ingredients. Shake to combine, then pour dressing over your favourite salad ingredients just before serving.

TIP
You can store any leftover dressing for up to a week in the fridge, tightly sealed in the jar. Remove the jar from the fridge a short while before you want it, and shake again before using.

Katherine Sabbath

Easy-peasy
Party Cake

Serves 10–12
Prep 30 minutes
+ 1 hour to soften butter

EQUIPMENT
mixing bowl, whisk, plastic wrap,
cake stand or large plate, A4-sized
sheet of non-stick baking paper,
non-toxic pencil, scissors, toothpick

INGREDIENTS

Maple Cream Cheese Icing
100 g unsalted butter
750 g (3 punnets) cream
   cheese
1 teaspoon vanilla bean
   paste
1 cup soft icing sugar
¼ cup maple syrup
   (you can also use honey)
1 tablespoon fresh lemon
   juice

Cake
2 cups (approx. ¾ batch)
   maple cream cheese icing
   (recipe to the left)
1 unfilled, double-layered
   vanilla sponge cake
   (look in the bakery aisle
   of your local supermarket)
a few drops of food
   colouring (optional)
1 cup of your favourite
   chocolates and
   confectionery
½ cup raspberry jam
1 cup rainbow sprinkles

Katherine says:
Get creative — when it comes to cake
decorating, the possibilities are only limited
by your own imagination!

1 First prepare the maple cream cheese
   icing. Take the butter out of the fridge
   about an hour before you need it, to
   allow it to come to room temperature
   and soften. Place the cream cheese in
   the mixing bowl and stir it with a spoon
   until it softens and is easier to mix.

2   Add the softened butter and beat the mixture with a whisk until smooth. If it is too hard to whisk easily, zap it in the microwave for 20 seconds on high to soften it. Add the vanilla bean paste, icing sugar, maple syrup, lemon juice and a few drops of food colouring (if using), and beat until light and fluffy. Cover with plastic wrap and set aside until needed.

3   To assemble the cake, place a small dollop of icing in the centre of your favourite cake stand or plate. Press one of the sponge cakes on top and press down, to give it grip. This will secure your cake to the plate.

4   Place a generous amount of icing on top of the cake, in the centre. Using a table knife, spread the icing over the top of the cake, slowly working towards the outside, until completely covered.

5   Stud the icing with an assortment of your favourite chocolates and confectionary. Mix the jam with a spoon to make it spreadable, then spoon a generous amount on top of the iced cake, in the centre. Spread the jam out, slowing working towards the outside edges.

6   Place the top layer of the cake on a separate plate and ice the top with the maple cream cheese icing. If the icing is really soft, place the cake in the fridge to let the icing harden for 20 minutes while you make your stencil.

7   Using the baking paper and pencil, draw the outline of any message you want, such as 'SWEET', 'EAT ME', 'HEY', etc. Or you can draw the outline of an object, such as a love heart, flower or a skull and crossbones. Use the scissors to cut out your design. Arrange the cut-out design on top of the top cake layer, lightly pressing down to secure it in place.

8   Next, hold your top cake over a large container or the kitchen sink — or save the mess and do this step outside! — and cover the top of the cake with a generous amount of rainbow sprinkles.

9   Use a toothpick to gently peel away the baking paper to reveal your custom design — and TA-DA! This cake is best enjoyed when served immediately.

Date Night

Justine Schofield

Crunchy
Chicken Schnitzel

Serves 2
Prep 15 minutes
Cook 10 minutes

EQUIPMENT
3 wide shallow bowls, baking paper, rolling pin, large non-stick frying pan, cooktop, non-scratch tongs or fish slice

INGREDIENTS

1 cup plain flour
2 teaspoons smoked paprika
2 teaspoons dried oregano
2 eggs
2 cloves garlic (optional)
2 cups panko breadcrumbs
½ cup grated parmesan
2 chicken breasts
4 tablespoons canola oil (or other neutral oil)
salt
lemon, to garnish

1 Set up a production line for crumbing your chicken using the 3 bowls. Place flour, paprika and oregano into the first bowl and stir to combine. Break the eggs into the second bowl and whisk with a fork. Grate the garlic cloves, if using, into the whisked egg.

2 Place breadcrumbs and parmesan into the third bowl (you could also spread them over a dinner plate) and stir to combine.

TIP
You can make your own breadcrumbs using stale bread – just blitz in a food processor. If using frozen bread, defrost and allow it to completely dry first.

3   Cut each chicken breast in half horizontally, to give two flatter pieces. Place each piece of chicken on a large sheet of baking paper and cover with a second sheet. Pound the chicken with the rolling pin to flatten it out, to about 1 cm thick (you could also use the back of the frying pan for this).

4   Coat a piece of chicken in the flour mixture, shake off any excess flour, then dip the piece in the egg mixture. Allow excess egg to drain off before transferring the piece to the bowl or plate with the crumb mixture. Press the chicken into the crumb mixture firmly, then turn to coat the other side. Set the crumbed chicken aside on a clean plate while you repeat the process with the other pieces.

5   Heat 2 tablespoons of oil in the large non-stick frying pan set over a medium to high heat. Put two pieces of crumbed chicken into the pan and cook on each side for 2 minutes, or until evenly golden-brown, turning them with the tongs or fish slice. To check that the chicken is cooked, make a little cut in the middle of one piece — it should be white all the way through.

6   Transfer the chicken onto a wire rack set over a baking tray or plate to rest. Add the remaining oil to the pan and cook the other two pieces of crumbed chicken the same way.

7   Serve with roasted vegetables (see page 191) or a tomato salad. Garnish with lemon wedges.

TIP
If you are a fan of the crumb, try double-crumbing! After coating each piece in crumb, return it to the bowl with the egg mixture. Allow excess to drain off, then transfer chicken back to the crumb mixture and coat again.

Mark LaBrooy

Maple-glazed
Pumpkin Salad

Seves 4
Prep 15 minutes
Cook 2 hours

EQUIPMENT
oven, ovenproof frying pan (or baking tray), baking paper, mixing bowl

INGREDIENTS

Pumpkin
½ whole pumpkin,
   cut horizontally
   (I used a Kent pumpkin)
2 tablespoons olive oil
4 tablespoons maple syrup
1 teaspoon flaked salt
   (or ½ tsp if using a salt
   grinder)
freshly ground black
   pepper
50 g goat's cheese
   (or haloumi)

Dressing
1 teaspoon Dijon mustard
   (use hot English or seeded
   mustard if preferred)
4 tablespoons olive oil
juice of ½ lemon
a pinch of salt
4 tablespoons apple cider
   vinegar

Salad
3 radishes
½ red onion
½ bunch mint leaves
1 bunch mixed salad leaves

1   Preheat the oven to 190°C. Line the ovenproof frying pan (or baking tray) with baking paper.

TIP
The other half of your pumpkin will keep for 2 weeks in the fridge if covered in plastic wrap. Cut off any manky bits before using.

2. Place the pumpkin half, cut-side up, in the pan or tray. Drizzle with half the oil and half the maple syrup, concentrating on the fleshy areas (the seeds in the middle will be scooped out and discarded later). Season generously with the flaked salt and freshly ground pepper, then roast in the oven for 2 hours.

3. Add all the dressing ingredients to a small bowl and whisk together with a spoon or fork. If you accidentally add too much vinegar, balance it out with extra olive oil. Set the dressing aside until you're ready to serve.

4. When the pumpkin is nearly ready, prepare the salad:
   - Trim both ends off the radishes. Slice into thin rounds and place in the mixing bowl.
   - Trim the top off the onion and cut it in half through the root. Remove the dry layers of skin, then cut each half into thin slices and add them to the bowl.
   - Pick the leaves off the bunch of mint and add them to the bowl.
   - Add the mixed salad leaves and set the salad aside.

5. When the pumpkin has finished roasting, remove it from the oven. Use a spoon to scoop out the seeds from the centre, leaving the base of the pumpkin in place. Transfer the pumpkin to a wooden board and drizzle with the remaining oil and maple syrup. Crumble the goat's cheese over the top.

6. Add the dressing to the salad and toss together gently — do this just before serving, to keep everything crisp. Serve the salad on top of the pumpkin, so that it's sitting in the bowl you created by scooping out the pumpkin seeds.

Justine Schofield

Crème Caramel

Serves 4
Prep 30 minutes
Cook 30 minutes
+ at least 2 hours chlling

EQUIPMENT
oven, 2 small saucepans, cooktop,
4 large oven-safe ramekins, large
mixing bowl, whisk, sieve, large jug,
deep roasting tray

INGREDIENTS
6 eggs (you will use 2 whole
 eggs and 4 yolks)
½ cup caster sugar
1 vanilla bean, or
 1 teaspoon vanilla extract
2 cups milk

Caramel
¾ cup caster sugar
3 tablespoons water

1   Preheat the oven to 160°C.

2   For the caramel, place the sugar and
water in a small saucepan and allow the
sugar to dissolve over a moderate heat.
To help the sugar dissolve, occasionally
swirl the pan in small circles — do not
stir the sugar mixture. Once it starts
to bubble, keep a close eye on it and
wait for the liquid to turn a deep
caramel colour.

3   Immediately remove the caramel from
the heat and pour one-third into each
large ramekin. Being careful not to touch
the caramel, gently swirl each ramekin
in small circles to ensure that the
caramel evenly coats the base and
reaches the edges at the bottom.

4

6

7

8

4   Tap one egg on the benchtop to crack the shell, then carefully break it open over a bowl — you are trying to let the egg white flow out while keeping the yolk in one half-shell. Tip the yolk into the large mixing bowl, and repeat with three more eggs. Break the last two eggs (whites and yolks) straight into the large bowl. Set the bowl of egg white aside for another use.

5   Add the sugar and whisk the eggs and sugar together until the mixture is thick and pale in colour.

6   If using the vanilla bean, slit it open down its length, open it up and scrape the seeds out. Place the milk and the vanilla in the other small saucepan and bring it to the boil, then pour it into the egg mixture while whisking continuously; this will ensure that the mixture will not split. Allow the custard mixture to rest for a minute or so, and then skim off any foam with a ladle or large metal spoon.

7   Strain the custard mixture through the sieve into the large jug. Place the ramekins in the deep roasting tray. Pour some custard into each ramekin on top of the caramel, stopping before you reach the top. Carefully add cold water to the tray to come about halfway up the ramekins.

8   Place the tray in the oven and cook for 30 minutes, or until the custard is set. It should be slightly jiggly in the middle but fairly firm around the edges. Once set, allow to cool completely and then place in the fridge to chill for a few hours, preferably overnight. You can make it up to three days in advance.

9   To serve, run a thin knife carefully around the edge of each ramekin. One at a time, place a shallow serving dish on top of the ramekin and flip the ramekin and dish over together. Gently shake until the custard de-moulds itself; the caramel will blanket the custard. Best served immediately.

Cheap As

Gregory Llewellyn

Greg's
Mac & Cheese

Serves 2
Prep 5 minutes
Cook 10 minutes

EQUIPMENT
5-litre stock pot, medium-sized
saucepan, cooktop, plastic wrap,
colander, serving bowl

INGREDIENTS
200 g elbow pasta
100 g butter
½ cup plain flour
½ teaspoon salt
freshly ground black pepper
2 cups milk
250 g grated Tasty cheese
100 ml white wine or beer
50 g of crumbly cheese

1 Put a stock pot of salted water on to boil.
Cook the pasta in the boiling water
according to the packet instructions
until al dente (just firm to the bite).

TIP
Be generous when
salting the pasta water.
You could add about
2 tablespoons to a
5-litre stockpot.

2   Melt the butter in the medium-sized saucepan over a
    low heat. When fully melted, add the flour and increase
    the heat to medium. Combine the butter and flour,
    stirring continuously; it should have the texture of
    loose, wet sand.

3   Stir in the salt and pepper, then add the milk in a steady
    stream while still stirring. Continue to stir constantly
    until the mixture boils, then turn the heat down to low
    and add the cheese. Cook on low until the cheese is
    melted, stirring often to ensure no sticking.

4   Add a little more milk if the sauce is too thick, and check
    the seasoning. Add the wine or beer, stir to combine and
    turn off the heat. Allow the sauce to cool a little.

5   Drain the cooked pasta and transfer it to a serving bowl.
    Add the cheese sauce and stir to combine. Sprinkle with
    the crumbly cheese before serving.

Monday Morning Cooking Club

Smashed Potatoes

Serves 6–8 as a side
Prep 20 minutes
Cook 1 hour

EQUIPMENT
oven, baking tray, baking paper, saucepan,
cooktop, potato masher (optional)

INGREDIENTS
1 kg baby (chat) potatoes
¼ cup olive oil
salt flakes

1   Preheat the oven to 180°C. Cover a
    baking tray with baking paper and
    set aside.

2   Place the potatoes in a saucepan and
    cover with cold water. Bring to the boil
    over a medium-high heat, and boil
    gently for 15-20 minutes until tender.
    When ready, a knife should easily
    pierce the potato. Drain and set aside
    to cool slightly.

3   Lay the potatoes on the baking tray.
    Using a potato masher, or the heel of
    your hand (covered with a clean tea
    towel if they're still very hot), gently
    smash each potato.

TIP
You can amp this
up by adding chilli flakes,
lemon zest, herbs or
even bacon to the tray
before roasting.

4 Drizzle over the olive oil and season liberally with salt.

5 Roast for 1 hour, or until the potatoes are dark-golden
   and crispy.

Monty Koludrovic

Monty's
Multinational Mussels

Serves 2
Prep 6 minutes
Cook 5–6 minutes

EQUIPMENT
2 large bowls, small-holed grater
or microplane, large deep cooktop
pan with tight-fitting lid, cooktop,
sandwich press or non-stick
frying pan

INGREDIENTS
1 clove garlic
3 cm piece ginger
1 shallot
1 small Lebanese
  cucumber
5 cm piece leek
a handful of your favourite
  herbs — parsley and basil
  is a great combo
1 bunch spinach
¼ small fresh chilli
  (optional)

1 kg mussels
  (I like XL ones)
200 ml (10 tablespoons)
  dry white wine
30 ml olive oil
½ lemon
50 g butter, diced
4 slices ciabatta or
  sourdough bread
extra virgin olive oil
  (or butter)
salt flakes and freshly
  ground black pepper

Monty says:
This dish may not be an every-night affair,
but it is a great one-pot wonder and it
features three amazing things: budget
seafood, good bread and real booze! When
I was living in London I would shop at the
Portobello Road Market a few times a week
and cook dishes like this for lunch with my
roomy. Like all cooking, you are rewarded
for buying fresh, good-quality produce to
start with, and it's often cheaper than the
supermarkets. Make sure you have an extra
bottle of wine for drinking too.

Mussels are great for entertaining and can
be fun to cook up outside on the barbecue or
over a fire! They're great all year round, easy
and — if nothing else — your mum will be
happy that you're eating more seafood!

1 Prepare the vegetables:
   - Peel and bruise the garlic, and peel and slice the ginger.
   - Trim the top off the shallot and cut it in half through the root. Remove the dry layers of skin, then slice each shallot half into small dice, discarding the root.
   - Halve the cucumber lengthways and slice it finely. Finely slice the leek.
   - Pick the leaves from the herbs and spinach, and set aside for later. If using the chilli, cut the stalk off, then cut down the length and open the chilli up. Remove the white parts and the seeds, then cut the chilli into fine strips and then very small dice.

2 Place the garlic, ginger, shallot, cucumber, leek and chilli (if using) in one of the large bowls together with the mussels, wine, olive oil, a scrape of zest from the lemon and a squeeze of lemon juice. Toss to combine.

3 Heat the large pan over a high heat, until almost smoking hot. Add the mussel mixture, place the lid on tightly and allow the mussels to steam open for 1 minute. Open the lid to check progress, and remove any open mussels to the other large bowl to one side. Cover the pan again to steam for 1 minute more, then check again and remove the open mussels. Repeat for another 1 minute. Discard any mussels that have not opened after 3 minutes.

4 Once all the mussels have been removed from the pan, dice the butter, add it to the sauce in the pan and shake until combined and emulsified.

5 After slicing the bread, I like to 'fry' my toast in a sandwich press . . . I always have a little one on the bench at home. It is just like having a toaster on your bench 24/7, which is the norm, but this way you can add olive oil or butter and go to the next level. It also does both sides at once and just needs a quick wipe to clean. If you don't have a sandwich press, use a non-stick frying pan to fry your bread.

6 Then just taste the sauce for seasoning. Usually the mussels will be salty enough, but you might need another squeeze of lemon juice. Add the herbs and spinach, and stir until softened. Return the mussels to the pan to heat through, stirring.

7 When warmed through, pour the mussels and sauce into a bowl, top with the toast and dig in.

Brigitte Hafner

Dead Simple Pancakes

Serves 2
Prep 2 minutes
Cook 3–5 minutes

EQUIPMENT
mixing bowl, whisk, non-stick frying
pan, cooktop, non-scratch fish slice

INGREDIENTS
4 heaped tablespoons
  self-raising flour
2 large (60 g) eggs
1 tablespoon plain yoghurt
a splash of milk
a pinch of salt
1 tablespoon butter

Topping ideas
· maple syrup
· Grand Marnier
· apricot jam

Brigitte says:
Dad's pancakes were quite special — and
slightly naughty. Every now and then he
would proclaim that today was a pancake
breakfast day, and would set up an electric
frying pan at the table so that he could flip
one hot pancake straight onto our waiting
plates. The reason they tasted so good was
because he used an outrageously big blob
of butter — the pancake would swim in
delicious browned foam — and as soon as
he had flipped a side he would sprinkle it
with a little Grand Marnier and smear it
with apricot jam. They were the best!

1   Place the flour, eggs and yoghurt in the
    mixing bowl and whisk together with just
    enough milk to make a thick batter. Once
    there are no more lumps, add a little
    more milk to make the batter runny but
    still thick.

2 Set the bowl aside to rest for 10 minutes.

3 Place the non-stick frying pan over a medium heat and add a generous knob of butter. When the butter has melted and is foaming, add a ladleful of the batter. If you don't have a ladle, use a small cup.

4 Cook until the underneath has firmed up and turned golden-brown (check by carefully lifting one edge with the fish slice), then flip once to finish cooking the other side.

5 Transfer the cooked pancake to a plate, and cover it with a clean tea towel to keep it warm while you cook the remaining pancakes. Serve with maple syrup or, as in our house, with a wee splash of Grand Marnier and apricot jam!

Fast Food

Dan Hong

Pimped-up Noodles

Serves 1
Prep 2 minutes
Cook 5 minutes

EQUIPMENT
small saucepan, cooktop, colander,
1 large and 1 small non-stick frying
pan, kitchen scissors

INGREDIENTS
1 Continental frankfurter sausage
¼ cup kimchi
1 single-serve packet instant noodles
1 tablespoon butter
2 tablespoons vegetable oil
1 egg
¾ cup grated cheddar cheese

1   Slice the frankfurter into rounds and
roughly chop the kimchi.

2   Bring a small saucepan of water to the boil. Cook the instant noodles in the boiling water for 2 minutes, or until al dente (just firm to the bite). Drain in a colander, then tip into a bowl of cold water to refresh. Drain again and set aside in the colander.

3   Place the large non-stick frying pan over a medium heat, then add the butter and allow it to melt and heat up. Add the frankfurter slices and kimchi, and sauté (fry gently) for 2 minutes.

4   Add the noodles and the noodle flavour sachets. Toss everything to combine, then use a pair of kitchen scissors to chop the noodles up a little.

5   Place the small non-stick frying pan over a medium heat, add the vegetable oil and let it heat up. Don't skimp on the oil — it sounds like a lot, but it really helps to get the egg super-crispy. Tap the egg on the benchtop to crack the shell, then break it into the hot oil. Fry the egg until the edges start to crisp up. To help the egg white cook, tip the pan and spoon hot oil over the white. When the egg white is almost set, carefully sprinkle the grated cheese around the outside of the egg and cook until the cheese is crispy and golden but the egg yolk is still soft. Place the noodles on a plate and top with the fried cheesy egg to serve.

③

⑤

⑤

Gregory Llewellyn

Last-minute
Pasta

Serves 2
Prep 5 minutes
Cook 10 minutes

EQUIPMENT
large saucepan, cooktop, large deep
frying pan, colander, small-holed
grater or microplane

INGREDIENTS

3 cloves garlic
a handful of mixed parsley
  and basil leaves
4 anchovy fillets
a handful of pitted olives
95 g can of tuna in chilli oil
salt
500 g packet pasta
  (spaghetti or whatever
  you have)
50 ml (2½ tablespoons)
  extra virgin olive oil,
  or use the oil from the
  tuna for extra heat

a splash of white wine —
  whatever you're drinking
  — or just some of the
  pasta water
2 teaspoons red chilli flakes
2 tablespoons butter
freshly ground black pepper
1 lemon
1-2 tablespoons finely
  grated Parmesan cheese

1 Prepare the ingredients — if everything
   is ready, the timing of the pasta sauce
   will equal the timing of the pasta.
   • Trim the bottoms off the garlic cloves,
     remove the skin and chop the garlic
     into thin slices.
   • Roughly chop the herbs and anchovy
     fillets (keep them separate).
   • Place the olives on a board and chop
     them into small pieces, or use the side
     of a large chopping knife to roughly
     crush them.
   • Open the can of tuna and drain the oil
     off into a cup.

2   Bring a large saucepan of heavily salted water to the boil, and add the pasta. Ensure that it is all submerged in the water, give it a stir and leave to boil, uncovered, while you make the sauce.

3   While the pasta is cooking, heat the frying pan over a medium heat. Add the olive oil or the same amount of the saved chilli oil, then the garlic, and stir-fry the garlic for 1 minute or until golden-brown. Add the parsley and basil leaves and fry until crisp. Add the anchovies and olives, and continue to cook for 2 minutes or until fragrant.

4   Add the wine (or a splash of the pasta water), chilli flakes, butter and shitloads of freshly ground black pepper, tossing to combine. Lower the heat to a simmer.

5   Drain the pasta in the colander, keeping about half a cup of the cooking water. Add the pasta and the half cup of cooking water to the frying pan, add the tuna and toss to combine.

6   Place the pasta in a serving bowl and grate a little lemon zest over it. Top with grated Parmesan.

Bernard Chu

Cake in a Mug

Serves 2
Prep 5 minutes
Cook 3–5 minutes

EQUIPMENT
1 large microwave-safe mug,
2 standard-sized microwave-safe
mugs (optional), 2 small microwave-
safe bowls or mugs, microwave

INGREDIENTS
70 g (just under ½ cup)
    self-raising flour
15 g (about 1 tablespoon)
    cocoa powder
20 g (5 teaspoons) caster
    sugar
a pinch of salt

1 egg
1 tablespoon butter
40 ml (2 tablespoons) milk
20 g (about 2 tablespoons)
    chocolate buttons or
    3 chocolate truffles
ice cream, to serve

Bernard says:
This recipe serves 2. You can make the
whole thing in one large mug and share it
with a friend, or you can split the mixture
into 2 separate mugs when you're halfway
through (see step 3).

1   Add the flour, cocoa, caster sugar
    and salt to the large mug. Crack the
    egg straight into the mug, then stir
    together until just combined.

2   Place the butter in one of the small
    microwave-safe bowls. Microwave
    on high for 10 seconds at a time,
    until melted.

TIP
This recipe uses caster
sugar because it's easier to
melt. You could replace it
with raw sugar, or leave the
sugar out completely and
add more ice cream!

③

④

3 Add the melted butter and milk to the mug and stir until well combined and smooth. You need to allow room for the cake to rise, so the mixture shouldn't come too close to the rim — your mug should be no more than two-thirds full. If you want to make 2 individual servings, you could transfer the mixture into 2 smaller mugs at this point.

4 Place the mug in the microwave (if you are using 2 mugs, be sure to microwave them one at a time). Microwave on high for 1 minute 30 seconds, then in short bursts of 10–30 seconds at a time until the cake rises. You don't need to worry too much about the cake being 'done'. If it's a little undercooked, you can call it a fondant, which is a yummy dessert with a liquid centre. If it's overcooked, it will be more like a brownie — these have a firmer, drier texture.

5 To make a chocolate sauce, place the chocolate buttons or truffles in the other small bowl or mug. Microwave on high for 30 seconds, then in 10-second bursts until the chocolate is melted, stirring after each burst.

6 Serve the cake with a scoop of ice cream, if desired. Pour the chocolate sauce over the top and eat straight away.

⑥

Home Takeaway

Christine Manfield

Veggie Dahl Curry

Serves 4
Prep 1 hour
Cook 25 minutes

EQUIPMENT
fine-holed grater, vegetable peeler, small saucepan, cooktop, frying pan, wooden spoon, large heavy-based saucepan, small sieve

INGREDIENTS
1½ cups chana dahl
  (or use split yellow lentils)
2 onions
4 cloves garlic
6 large green chillies
3 cm piece ginger
⅓ butternut pumpkin
1 medium sweet potato
½ head cauliflower
1 teaspoon coriander seeds
2½ tablespoons sunflower
  oil
1 teaspoon fenugreek seeds
1 teaspoon brown mustard
  seeds
12 fresh curry leaves
1 teaspoon ground
  turmeric
½ tsp chilli flakes
  (optional)
400 ml can of coconut milk
1 lemon
½ bunch coriander
salt flakes
4 cups steamed basmati
  rice (see page 44), to serve

1   Wash the dahl thoroughly. Place in a bowl, cover with cold water and leave to soak for 30 minutes, then drain through a sieve.

2   While the dahl is soaking, prepare the vegetables.
  · Trim the tops off the onions and cut each in half through the root. Remove the dry layers of skin, then chop each onion half into small dice, discarding the root.
  · Trim the bottoms off the garlic cloves, remove the skin and chop the garlic into thin slices and then small pieces.
  · Cut the stalks off the chillies, then cut down each length and open the chillies up. Remove the white parts and seeds, then cut the chilli into thin strips and then very small dice.
  · Peel the ginger, then grate it on a fine-holed grater.
  · Peel the butternut pumpkin and sweet potato, then cut into 2 cm cubes.
  · Remove any green leaves from the cauliflower, then cut it into small pieces, discarding the base of the stalk.

(4)

(4)

3   Bring a small saucepan of water to the boil, add the dahl
    and simmer for about 10 minutes or until just cooked
    through.

4   Place a dry frying pan over a low heat, then add the
    coriander seeds and stir with a wooden spoon until they
    are fragrant (this should take 1–2 minutes). Tip onto a
    plate to cool completely, then grind to a powder. If you
    don't have a spice grinder, place the seeds in a ziplock
    bag, seal the bag, then bash it with a wooden rolling pin
    until crushed.

5   Heat the sunflower oil in the large, heavy-based saucepan
    on a medium-high heat, and fry the fenugreek and
    mustard seeds for about 30 seconds, until the seeds
    splutter and change colour.

6   Add the onion, garlic, green chilli, ginger, curry leaves
    and turmeric and fry for 3-4 minutes, until the onion
    has softened and taken on a little colour. Add the ground
    coriander seeds and chilli flakes (if using), then the
    coconut milk and 1 cup of water. Stir to combine, then
    add the remaining vegetables.

7   Reduce the heat to medium and bring the curry to a
    gentle boil. Simmer for 15 minutes, or until the vegetables
    are al dente (just firm to the bite), then add the cooked
    dahl. Cook for a further 10 minutes, until the vegetables
    and dahl are soft but still holding their shape.

8   Meanwhile, cut the lemon in half and squeeze it through
    the sieve into a small bowl. Pick the leaves off the sprigs
    of coriander.

9   Season the curry with lemon juice and salt, to taste.
    Remove the pan from the heat and stir in the coriander
    leaves. Serve with steamed basmati rice (see page 44).

Martin Boetz

Stir-fried Rice Noodles

Serves 2
Prep 10 minutes
Cook 10 minutes

EQUIPMENT
wok or large frying pan, cooktop

INGREDIENTS
1 small onion
½ bunch bok choy
2–3 cm piece fresh ginger
1 long red chilli (optional)
2 green shallot stalks
1 lime
200 g beef rump or topside
3 tablespoons coconut or
   vegetable oil
300 g fresh rice noodles
a pinch of white sugar
4 tablespoons oyster sauce
5 tablespoons chicken
   stock
a handful of coriander or
   Thai basil leaves
a pinch of white pepper
1 tablespoon fried onions
   (from Asian grocers),
   to serve

1   Prepare the ingredients:
   · Trim the top off the onion and cut it
     in half through the root. Remove the
     dry layers of skin, then slice each half
     lengthways.
   · Wash the bok choy and cut it into
     quarters through the stalk.
   · Peel the ginger and slice it into thin
     strips.
   · If using the chilli, slice it finely into
     rounds (seeds and all), discarding
     the stalk.
   · Finely slice the shallot stalks and cut
     the lime into wedges. Set them aside
     for serving.
   · Slice the beef thinly across the grain.
     (The grain is the direction in which
     the meat fibres run. Always slice
     across the grain rather than parallel
     with it.)

TIP
A wok is cheap to buy,
and as long as you
keep it clean and oiled
between uses, you'll
have it forever.

2   Heat the wok over a high heat. Add the onion and dry-fry
    it for 1–2 minutes until slightly charred on the edges.
    Add the oil, then the beef, allowing it to brown slightly
    for 2–3 minutes, turning it once or twice to ensure a deep
    and even colour.

3   Throw in the bok choy, noodles and chilli (if using),
    tossing the ingredients to mix. Add in the sugar, oyster
    sauce and then the stock, and stir to coat the meat and
    vegetables. Add in the ginger, stir to combine and then
    take the wok off the heat.

4   Garnish with sliced green shallots, coriander or Thai
    basil leaves, white pepper and fried onions. Serve
    immediately, with lime wedges to squeeze over.

Daniel Wilson

Dan's Best At-home Burgers

Serves 4
Prep 15 minutes
Cook 10 minutes

EQUIPMENT
mixing bowl, baking paper, saucepan,
2 non-stick frying pans, cooktop
(or barbecue with hotplate), fish slice

INGREDIENTS

2 tomatoes
4 leaves iceberg lettuce
500 g beef mince
salt and freshly ground
  black pepper
8 rashers bacon
4 sesame burger buns
vegetable oil, for frying

4 slices cheddar cheese
4 eggs
tomato sauce
good-quality egg
  mayonnaise
sliced pickles
yellow mustard
8 slices canned beetroot

1   Slice the tomatoes into rounds. Wash the
lettuce leaves, gently pat dry with paper
towels and tear into three or four pieces.
Set the tomato and lettuce aside.

TIP
Choose mince with
a slightly higher fat content
to give your patties texture.
If you can only find lean
mince, you could cut some
of the fatty bits off the
bacon and mix them
through the mince.

2   Place the mince in the mixing bowl, season generously with salt and pepper, and use clean hands to mix well. Divide the mince into 4 balls, placing each on a sheet of baking paper.

3   Place a second sheet of baking paper on top of the meat. Use the bottom of the saucepan to flatten the patties to about ½ cm thick and about twice the size of the burger buns (the patties will shrink when cooking). Set aside.

4   Heat the non-stick frying pan to a medium-high heat, and fry the bacon until crisp, turning it over occasionally. You can also use the flatplate on a barbecue.

5   Split the buns in half and place them cut-side down in the same pan to toast for 1–2 minutes. They should be slightly golden around the edges. Set them aside.

6   Add 1 tablespoon of oil to the same pan and cook the meat patties on one side for 3 minutes, then turn them over. Cook for 1 minute, then place a slice of cheese on each pattie. Cook for a further 2 minutes to allow the cheese to melt.

7   While the cheese is melting, fry the eggs. Add 2 tablespoons of oil to the second frying pan over a medium-high heat. Allow the oil to heat up, then tap each egg in turn on the benchtop to crack the shell, and break it open into the pan. Cook the eggs until the white has set but the yolk is still runny. To help the white set, tip the pan slightly and spoon some hot oil over the egg whites.

8 Spread some tomato sauce on the cut side of the bun bottom and some mayonnaise on the cut side of the bun top. Build your burger from the bottom up in this order: bun bottom with tomato sauce, pickles, pattie with cheese, mustard, bacon, egg, beetroot, tomato, lettuce, bun top with mayonnaise. Eat immediately.

Neil Perry

Blue-eye Trevalla
Cooked in a Bag

Serves 4
Prep 15 minutes
Cook 10–12 minutes
+ 5 minutes resting

EQUIPMENT
oven, vegetable peeler, mixing bowl,
baking paper, baking tray

INGREDIENTS
1 green zucchini
1 yellow zucchini
2 shallots
¼ bunch tarragon
sea salt and freshly ground
    black pepper
4 tablespoons dry white
    wine

4 fillets blue-eye trevalla
    (180 g each)
2 tablespoons extra virgin
    olive oil
4 sprigs thyme
8 small bay leaves
40 g unsalted butter

---

1   Preheat the oven to 200°C.

2   Prepare the vegetables and herbs:
    · Slice the zucchinis into thin strips
      with the vegetable peeler.
    · Trim the top off each shallot and cut
      it in half through the root. Remove
      the dry layers of skin, then finely slice
      each half lengthways (about 3 mm
      wide).
    · Chop the tarragon — you will need
      1 tablespoon of chopped herb.

3   Place the zucchini and shallot in a bowl
    with the chopped tarragon, a little salt
    and pepper and the wine. Mix well.

(5)

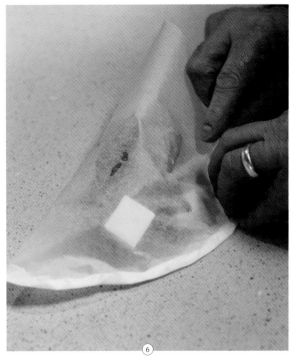

(6)

(6)

4   Tear off four pieces of baking paper about 30 cm long.
    Fold each in half, cut it into a semicircle and open up
    again to a circle. Divide the zucchini mixture between
    the paper circles, arranging it on one side of each circle
    in thin layers. Drizzle with any liquid left in the bowl.

5   Place a fish fillet on top of the vegetables. Season with
    salt and pepper and drizzle ½ tablespoon extra virgin
    olive oil over each fillet. Place a thyme sprig and 2 bay
    leaves on top. Cut the butter into cubes and add to the
    top of each fillet.

6   Fold the paper over the food, then start to fold the edges
    together tightly with closely overlapping little folds. Twist
    and fold the bottom end over. You should leave enough
    space around the food to allow the air to expand and
    circulate; it will swell up like a balloon during cooking.

7   Place the paper packets on the baking tray, and place in
    the hot oven. Bake for about 10-12 minutes, until the fish
    is just cooked through. If you're not sure, carefully open
    a corner of one parcel to check.

8   Remove from the oven and allow to rest for 5 minutes.
    Serve parcels unopened on plates so your guests can
    enjoy the hit of aroma as they open the parcels.

Comfort Food

Colin Fassnidge

Sticky
Lamb Ribs

Serves 2–3
Prep 20 minutes
+ overnight to marinate
Cook 2 hours, 35 minutes
+ 30 minutes resting

EQUIPMENT
mixing bowl, fine-holed grater (optional),
frying pan, cooktop, large and deep baking
tray, plastic wrap, oven, aluminium foil,
microwave-safe bowl, microwave

INGREDIENTS

thumb-sized piece of fresh
  ginger
2 long red chillies
375 ml can of cola
1 cup tomato sauce
1 cup barbecue sauce
4 tablespoons red wine
  vinegar (you can also use
  lemon juice or another
  vinegar)

4 tablespoons soy sauce
4 tablespoons Dijon
  mustard
2 cinnamon quills
4 star anise
2 lamb short rib racks
1 spring onion, to garnish
coriander leaves, to garnish

---

1   Peel the ginger, chop it into small
    pieces and place it in the mixing bowl.
    Alternatively, you could grate it using a
    fine-holed grater. Finely slice the chillies
    into rounds (seeds and all).

2   Add the cola, tomato and barbecue
    sauces, vinegar, soy sauce and mustard
    to the bowl of ginger, and stir to combine.
    Add most of the chilli and stir in. Set the
    remaining sliced chilli aside for a garnish.

3   Heat the frying pan over a high heat, then add the cinnamon and star anise. Swirl the pan around for 20 seconds, or until the spices are fragrant (no oil is needed). Add to the marinade mixture in the bowl and mix in.

4   Place the ribs in the large, deep baking tray. Pour two-thirds of the marinade mixture over the ribs, making sure they are well covered. Cover the tray and the remaining marinade with plastic wrap and refrigerate overnight.

5   Preheat the oven to 175°C. Remove the tray from the fridge, remove the plastic wrap and cover the ribs tightly with aluminium foil, placing the foil inside the baking tray. Set aside for 30 minutes at room temperature, then cook the ribs in the oven for 2½ hours or until the meat starts to fall off the bone. If the meat is still firm after this time, bake for a further 15 minutes or until tender.

6   Meanwhile, make the glaze. Place the reserved marinade in the microwave-safe bowl and zap on high for 3-4 minutes until thickened and bubbling.

7   When the ribs are tender, increase the oven temperature to 225°C. Remove the aluminium foil and brush the hot marinade onto the ribs. Cook, uncovered, for a further 10 minutes or until dark and sticky.

8   Rest the ribs for 30 minutes, then use a large knife to cut through the meat and separate the rack into individual ribs. Finely chop the spring onion into rounds, then use it to garnish the ribs along with the reserved chilli and the coriander leaves. Serve with a crisp green salad and a cold beer.

Anna Eoclidi

Anna's Classic
Lasagne

Serves 4–6
Prep 1 hour
Cook 1 hour

EQUIPMENT
large frying pan, cooktop, wooden
spoon, oven, large deep roasting tray
or lasagne dish, baking paper

INGREDIENTS

Ragù (meat sauce)
1 onion
1 carrot
1 stalk of celery
1 tablespoon olive oil
50 g butter
salt flakes
50 g pancetta or bacon
150 g coarse pork mince
150 g coarse veal mince
freshly ground black pepper
125 ml (½ cup) white wine
400 g can of chopped
  tomatoes
1 tablespoon tomato paste

To assemble
3 balls bocconcini cheese
  (optional)
2 cups grated firm
  mozzarella cheese
1 cup finely grated
  Parmesan cheese
400 g fresh lasagne sheets

Anna says:
Lasagne is a traditional Italian dish perfect
for serving when friends or family are over.
If you follow the recipe, you are guaranteed
a huge success.

1   Prepare the vegetables for the ragù:
    · Trim the top off the onion and cut it in
      half through the root. Remove the dry
      layers of skin, then chop each onion
      half into dice, discarding the root.
    · Peel the carrot, trim off both ends and
      cut the carrot in half lengthways. Cut
      each half into three or four long pieces
      and then into dice.
    · Trim the ends off the celery and cut
      it into strips and then dice.

2   Pour the oil into the large frying pan set over a medium
    heat. Add the butter, then add the chopped onion and a
    pinch of salt. Stir occasionally for 1-2 minutes, until the
    onion is starting to brown. Add the chopped carrots and
    celery and cook for 5 minutes, stirring occasionally.

3   While the vegetables are cooking, chop the pancetta or
    bacon into dice. Add to the pan and stir to mix. After
    1 minute, add the pork and veal mince. Cook the meat
    for 5-6 minutes until browned, stirring and breaking it
    up with a wooden spoon.

4   Season the meat mixture with salt and pepper and add
    the wine. Cook for 5 minutes to allow the alcohol to
    evaporate, then add the canned tomatoes and tomato
    paste and stir to combine. Reduce the heat to low and
    simmer the ragù for 30 minutes (but 1 hour is ideal),
    adding a splash of water if it starts to look dry.

5   To make the lasagne, preheat the oven to 180°C. Line the bottom of the roasting tray or lasagne dish with a sheet of baking paper. If using the bocconcini cheese, slice it thickly.

6   Spoon one-third of the ragù into the dish, covering the base completely. Cover this with one-third of the mozzarella and Parmesan cheese, then cover this with half the pasta, being careful not to overlap the sheets.

7   Repeat the previous step (ragù, then mozzarella and Parmesan, then pasta), then finish with the remaining ragù, mozzarella and Parmesan, and the bocconcini slices (if using).

8   Bake in the oven for 1 hour, or until golden on top and bubbling around the edges. Remove from the oven and leave to rest for 5 minutes, then cut into portions and serve. Buon appetito!

TIP
You can freeze leftover portions, well wrapped in plastic wrap, or refrigerate them to eat the next day. To defrost, place frozen lasagne in the fridge the night before you want to eat it. Reheat in an oven set to 160°C until a knife inserted into the centre comes out hot.

Daniel Wilson

Crispy-yet-chewy
Choc Chip Cookies

Makes 20
Prep 15 minutes
Cook 15 minutes

EQUIPMENT
oven, 2 mixing bowls, hand-held
electric beater (or a wooden spoon),
2 baking trays, baking paper, plastic
wrap, wire cooling rack

INGREDIENTS
250 g unsalted butter
2¾ cups plain flour
1½ teaspoons salt
1 teaspoon baking soda
1 teaspoon baking powder
¾ cup caster sugar

1¼ cups lightly packed
  brown sugar
2 large eggs
1 teaspoon vanilla extract
1½ cups dark chocolate
  chips (60% cocoa)

1   Take the butter out of the fridge about
    an hour before you want to start cooking,
    and chop it into largish cubes. Leave it to
    come to room temperature and soften.

2   Preheat the oven to 175°C. Sift the flour,
    salt, baking soda and baking powder
    together into the mixing bowl and
    set aside.

3   Place the butter and both types of sugar
    in a separate mixing bowl and beat them
    together until pale and fluffy. An electric
    beater is best for this, but a wooden
    spoon and elbow grease will also work.
    Scrape down the sides of the bowl a few
    times to ensure that all the butter is
    beaten in.

TIP
If you don't want to bake
all the cookies in one go, roll
the unused dough into a log, wrap
it in plastic wrap and store it in
the fridge for up to a month or the
freezer for up to 3 months. You
can slice the dough into rounds
straight from the fridge or
freezer and bake them
in a hot oven.

4   Add the eggs one at a time, beating them in well after
    each addition, then add the vanilla extract and beat in.

5   Add one-third of the sifted flour mixture and mix in.
    Repeat with the second third, then the last, until
    everything is combined into a sticky dough. Add the
    chocolate chips and fold in with a wooden spoon.

6   Cover 2 baking trays with baking paper. Using a
    tablespoon, scoop 1 spoonful per cookie onto the tray,
    leaving room between each cookie so they can spread out
    during baking. You should be able to fit 4-6 cookies on
    each tray. Cover any unused dough with plastic wrap
    until you're ready to bake it (see the tip on the previous
    page also).

7   Bake batches of cookies for 15 minutes, or 7-8 minutes
    if you are using a fan-forced oven. The cookies should
    be golden and crisp around the edges when done. Allow
    the cookies to cool slightly on the trays, then transfer
    them to the wire cooling rack. Let the trays cool a little
    more before baking the next batch.

Sunday Nights

Nathan Sasi

Roast Chicken
with Real Gravy

Serves 4
Prep 30 minutes
Cook 1 hour

EQUIPMENT
oven, paper towels, roasting
tray, wooden spoon, saucepan,
cooktop, whisk

INGREDIENTS

1.4 kg chicken	1 bunch rosemary
1 small head of garlic,	1 bunch thyme
plus 4 extra cloves	2 bay leaves
2 carrots	olive oil
1 leek	¾ cup white wine
1 onion	1 cup boiling water
1 lemon	1 tablespoon soy sauce
salt flakes	1 teaspoon tomato paste
freshly ground black pepper	1 tablespoon cornflour

1   Preheat the oven to 220°C. Remove the
chicken from the fridge and set it aside
for 30 minutes at room temperature.

2   Prepare the vegetables:
  • Slice the top off the head of garlic.
  Smash the extra unpeeled garlic cloves
  with the flat side of a large chopping
  knife to crush them a little.
  • Peel the carrots and chop them into
  thickish rounds.
  • Trim the dark green part off the leek,
  then wash it thoroughly and chop it
  into thickish rounds.
  • Trim the top off the onion and cut it
  in half through the root. Remove the
  dry layers of skin, then roughly chop
  the rest, discarding the root.
  • Cut the lemon into quarters.

3   Wash the chicken under cold running
water, then pat dry with paper towels.
Season the outside of the chicken with
salt and pepper, then place the quartered
lemon, smashed garlic cloves and half
each of the rosemary and thyme inside
the cavity. Drizzle the chicken with a
little olive oil and spread it all over the
skin with your fingers.

(4)

(5)

4   Place the carrot, leek, head of garlic, onion and bay
    leaves in a roasting tray. Drizzle over a really good lug
    of olive oil, season with salt and toss to coat.

5   Place the chicken, breast side up, directly onto the oven
    rack. Place the tin of vegetables directly underneath,
    to catch the chicken juices. Roast the chicken and
    vegetables for 45 minutes. The chicken is cooked when
    the juices run clear when you pierce the leg joint with
    a skewer or sharp knife. If the juices are still pink, roast
    for a further 10 minutes, then check again.

6   Once cooked, set the chicken aside on a plate or tray for
    20 minutes while you make the gravy — this is the secret
    to a juicy chicken.

7   For the gravy, remove two-thirds of the vegetables from the tin and set them aside for serving. Pour the wine into the roasting tray and use a wooden spoon or spatula to scrape up the crispy bits from the bottom. Bring a kettle to the boil and pour 1 cup of just-boiled water into the roasting tray, continuing to scrape.

8   Transfer the contents of the tin to a saucepan, set it over a medium-high heat and bring it to the boil. Turn the heat down and simmer for 10 minutes, until the liquid has reduced by a third, then add the soy sauce and tomato paste. Stir well to combine, and continue to simmer for 10 minutes.

9   Use a slotted spoon to remove the solids from the gravy. Or, if you want a super-smooth gravy, strain the gravy through a sieve and then add it back to the saucepan. Pour any resting juices from the chicken into the gravy.

10 In a cup, mix the cornflour with a splash (about 30 ml) of water. Slowly stir the cornflour mixture into the simmering gravy, and continue to whisk for 30 seconds or until the gravy thickens. Season with salt and pepper to taste, and serve warm with the roast chicken and vegetables.

(7)

(7)

(8)

(9)

(10)

Jill Dupleix

Jill's Amazing
Potato Mash

Serves 2 as a side
Prep 10 minutes
Cook 20 minutes

EQUIPMENT
large saucepan, cooktop,
potato masher, wooden spoon

INGREDIENTS
5 medium potatoes — red-skinned ones work well
sea salt and freshly ground black pepper
1-2 tablespoons cold butter
150 ml milk

For best results, the butter should be cold and the milk hot.

1 Peel the potatoes and halve them. Place them in a large saucepan and cover with cold water. Add a good pinch of salt and then bring the water to the boil over a medium-high heat. Once boiling, reduce the heat and gently simmer for 20 minutes or until the potatoes are tender. Best way to tell? Stick a bamboo skewer in one and lift it. If the potato drops off, it's cooked.

TIP
Don't cut your potatoes too small, as they will absorb too much water. Watery potato won't mash into a smooth texture.

3

2   While the potatoes are cooking, chop the butter into smallish pieces.

3   Drain the potatoes well and return them to the dry saucepan to dry out for 10 seconds or so. Mash the potatoes with force — beat them to a pulp.

4   Use a wooden spoon to make a well (a hole) in the centre, and pour in the milk, then beat in well with the wooden spoon. Add the butter and some sea salt and pepper, beating well until the mash is smooth and glossy. Add more milk to lighten it if need be.

5   Serve hot. If you wish, top with a little extra butter and grind over some extra black pepper.

TIP
For a change of flavour, heat the milk with 1 crushed garlic clove, or a finely diced onion, or chopped spring onions. Swap the butter for extra virgin olive oil.

Bernard Chu

Mixed
Berry Crumble

Serves 4
Prep 15 minutes
+ 20 minutes resting
Cook 20 minutes

EQUIPMENT
sieve, mixing bowl, oven, oven-safe
ramekins, baking tray

INGREDIENTS

⅔ cup plain flour
100 g unsalted butter
⅓ cup caster sugar
½ cup almond meal
a pinch of salt

pure icing sugar, to taste
500 g packet frozen mixed
   berries (no need to defrost)
ice cream (optional)

1   Sift the flour into a mixing bowl. Cut the
    butter into cubes and add to the bowl.
    With clean, dry hands, pick up small
    amounts of flour and butter, and rub
    them between your fingertips to combine
    a little.

TIP
For a variation, try
adding ground cinnamon
to your crumble mix. You
could also use ground
cardamom.

2 Continue rubbing small amounts of butter and flour together until the entire mixture has a breadcrumb texture. Add the caster sugar, almond meal and salt, and stir in. Place the bowl in the fridge to rest for 15 to 20 minutes. You can also make the crumble mixture the night before.

3 Preheat the oven to 180°C. Mix some icing sugar with the mixed berries, and spoon the berries into individual ramekins. Top each ramekin with the crumble mixture.

4 Place the ramekins on the baking tray and bake for about 20 minutes, or until golden and bubbling around the edges. Garnish with some extra icing sugar dusted on top. Serve with a scoop of ice cream if you wish.

Meat Fest

Hayden Quinn

Crispy Crackling Pork
with Apple Slaw

Serves 6–8
Prep 25 minutes
+ overnight, to dry
out the skin
Cook 4½ hours
+ 20 minutes resting

EQUIPMENT
baking tray, large plastic container
(optional), oven, large mixing bowl

INGREDIENTS

Crispy pork shoulder
2.5 kg boneless pork
    shoulder, skin on
½ cup salt flakes (regular
    salt will also work)
2 teaspoons Chinese
    five-spice powder

Slaw
½ wombok cabbage
2 Granny Smith apples

½ cup unsalted, roasted
    peanuts
1 long green chilli
½ bunch coriander
2 tablespoons apple cider
    vinegar
2 tablespoons extra virgin
    olive oil
salt and freshly ground
    black pepper

1   Lay pork shoulder, skin-side up, on a
    chopping board. Using a sharp knife,
    carefully score the skin at 1 cm intervals.
    Be careful not to cut completely through
    the fat, as the meat can dry out if you do.

2   Place the salt and five-spice powder in a
    small bowl, and toss together to combine.
    Rub two-thirds of the salt mix into the
    skin and score lines. Flip the pork over
    and rub the remaining salt mix into
    the flesh.

3 Transfer the pork, skin-side up, to the baking tray or a plastic container large enough to hold it when laid flat. Refrigerate, uncovered, for at least 6 hours (or overnight), as this helps the skin dry out.

4 When ready to cook, preheat the oven to 160°C. Remove the pork from the fridge and set it aside for 20 minutes to allow it to come to room temperature. Transfer the pork (if necessary) to the baking tray and roast it for 3½ hours. If the skin starts to burn on the edges, cover those areas with aluminium foil.

5 After the 3½ hours, increase the oven temperature to 200°C and roast for a final 30 minutes, or until the crackling puffs up slightly and makes a hollow sound when tapped. Remove the pork from the oven and set it aside, uncovered, to rest for 20 minutes while you make the slaw. The crackling will continue to harden while resting.

6 Finely slice the wombok width-ways, then transfer it to the large mixing bowl. Cut the apples in half from top to bottom, then slice them thinly, discarding the cores. Stack the slices and cut them into matchsticks. Add the apple to the wombok, along with the peanuts.

7 Finely slice the chilli into rounds and add them to the slaw. Pick the leaves from the sprigs of coriander. Leave a few aside for a garnish, then roughly chop the rest and add them to the slaw. Pour in the vinegar and oil, then, with clean hands, mix the salad ingredients to combine. Season with salt and pepper to taste, and garnish with the extra coriander leaves.

8 Serve the pork on a board, carving generous slices at the table. Serve the slaw on the side.

Jill Dupleix

Slashed Roast Leg of Lamb

Serves 4–6
Prep 15 minutes
Cook 1 hour 20 minutes
+ 10 minutes resting

EQUIPMENT
oven, mixing bowl, grater,
kitchen string, large roasting tray,
aluminium foil

INGREDIENTS
½ bunch parsley and/or
   mint
2 anchovies in oil
   (optional)
3 cloves garlic
2 lemons
2 teaspoons salted baby
   capers, drained

about 4 slices sourdough
   or other firm, non-grainy
   bread
3 tablespoons extra virgin
   olive oil, plus extra to
   drizzle
1 leg of lamb (approx. 2 kg)

1   Preheat the oven to 220°C.

2   Prepare the stuffing:
   • Roughly chop the herbs and anchovies,
      and place in the mixing bowl.
   • Trim the bottoms off the garlic cloves,
      remove the skin and then crush the
      cloves with the flat side of a large
      chopping knife, or grate them, and
      add them to the bowl.
   • Finely grate the zest from one of the
      lemons, and add this to the bowl.
   • Add the capers to the bowl.
   • Grate the bread slices into breadcrumbs,
      discarding the crusts. You want to end
      up with 1½ cups of fresh breadcrumbs.
      Add these to the bowl with the
      3 tablespoons of olive oil.
   • Using your hands, squish everything
      together to form a mushy paste.

3   Hold the leg of lamb with its meatiest side on top and cut right through the meat, almost to the bone, at 2 cm intervals. Push the stuffing down between each cut, then reshape the meat into a leg shape and use kitchen string to tie it all together. Place the lamb in the large roasting tray.

4   Drizzle a little extra olive oil over the top of the lamb, and roast for 20 minutes. Reduce the heat to 200°C and roast for a further 1 hour, then remove from the oven, cover loosely with aluminium foil and set aside for 10 minutes to rest.

5   Cut the second lemon into wedges. Remove the string from the lamb and carve the meat parallel to the bone, to form chunky pieces of crisp skin and meat. Pour over the roasting juices from the tin and serve with the lemon wedges to squeeze over.

TIP
If your leg of lamb was a different weight to start with, follow this rule for the roasting time: after the first 20 minutes, allow 30 minutes per kilo to ensure that your lamb is cooked properly.

Anthony Puharich

Rump Steak
with Chimichurri Sauce

Serves 3
Prep 1 minute
Cook about 6 minutes
+ 2 minutes resting

EQUIPMENT
barbecue hotplate or heavy-based
frying pan, aluminium foil

INGREDIENTS
1 rump steak (400–500 g), at least 2 cm thick
3 tablespoons olive oil
sea salt
chimichurri sauce (see page 187) or mustard, to serve

1   Cut the steak into portions of the desired size. Rub each steak with a tablespoon of olive oil and a good pinch of sea salt.

TIP
Take the meat out of the fridge at least 15 minutes before you cook it. Meat at room temperature cooks more evenly.

2   Heat the hotplate of the barbecue or a heavy-based frying
    pan to a high heat. Once hot, add the steak. Cook for
    6 minutes for medium-rare, or to your liking, turning the
    steak over every minute.

3   Once cooked to your liking, transfer the steak to a plate
    or board and loosely cover with aluminium foil. Leave to
    rest for 2 minutes.

4   Using a sharp knife, slice the steak across the grain. Serve
    with the resting juices drizzled on top and your favourite
    mustard or chimichurri sauce on the side.

Anthony Puharich

Chimichurri Sauce

Makes about 2 cups
Prep 10 minutes

EQUIPMENT
Blender

INGREDIENTS

3 cloves garlic
1 shallot
½ bunch coriander
½ bunch flat-leaf parsley
½ small bunch oregano
¼ cup red wine vinegar

2 teaspoons salt flakes
2 teaspoons sliced pickled
  jalapeño chillies
¾ cup extra virgin olive oil
salt and freshly ground
  black pepper

1   Prepare the ingredients:
    · Trim the bottom off the garlic cloves,
      remove the skin and then crush the
      cloves with the flat side of a large
      chopping knife.
    · Trim the top off the shallot and cut it
      in half through the root. Remove the
      dry layers of skin, then cut each half
      in half again, through the root. Trim
      off the root.
    · Remove the stalks from the coriander
      and parsley, and roughly chop the
      leaves. Pick the leaves off the sprigs
      of oregano, discarding the stems.

2   Place the vinegar, salt, garlic, shallot
    and jalapeño chilli in a bowl and leave
    to stand for 5 minutes.

3   Transfer chilli mixture to the blender
    and add coriander, parsley, oregano
    and oil.

4   Whiz to combine, then taste and adjust
    seasoning with salt and pepper if
    necessary.

5   Pour into a serving bowl. May be stored
    in a sterilised jar or container in the
    fridge for up to a week.

Fit & Healthy

Alice Zaslavsky

Roast Vegetables

Serves 4
Prep 20 minutes
Cook 1 hour

EQUIPMENT
oven, aluminium foil, large and deep
roasting tray

INGREDIENTS

1 whole head garlic
1 head broccoli
1 bunch asparagus
2 onions
2 capsicums
2 medium carrots
4 potatoes

1 small sweet potato
½ butternut pumpkin
2 beetroots
1 bunch thyme or
   marjoram sprigs
olive oil
salt flakes

1   Preheat the oven to 180°C.

2   Prepare the vegetables:
   · Trim the top off the head of garlic.
     Chop the broccoli into medium-sized
     florets. Snap the woody part off the
     bottoms of the asparagus spears and
     discard.
   · Trim the top off the onion and cut it in
     half through the root. Remove the dry
     layers of skin, then cut each half into
     three pieces.
   · Cut the stalk and core out of the
     capsicums, then cut them in half and
     remove the white parts and any seeds.
     Cut the capsicum into thick strips and
     then large dice.
   · Peel the carrots and cut them into
     thick rounds.
   · Peel the potatoes, sweet potato and
     butternut pumpkin, and chop them
     into smallish pieces a little bigger
     than the carrot rounds.

3   Wash the beetroots and trim off the tops
    and bottoms. Place each beetroot on
    a square of aluminium foil big enough to
    wrap it completely. Drizzle with olive oil
    and wrap each beetroot tightly.

TIP
Cook a couple of
extra heads of garlic to
keep in the fridge for other
recipes, like the veggie
salad on page 193.

4   Place all the vegetables except the beetroot parcels in a large, deep roasting tray. Scatter the herbs over the vegetables and drizzle everything with olive oil and a good few pinches of salt. Toss the vegetables to coat them in oil. Add the beetroot to the tin.

5   Place the tin of vegetables in the oven. Roast for 1 hour, or until the vegetables are soft and have taken on some colour. Halfway through the cooking time, remove the tin from the oven and toss the vegetables so that they will cook evenly.

6   Set aside to cool slightly, then squeeze the soft garlic cloves out of their skins on top of the vegetables. Toss gently, season with a little more salt, and serve. Leftover roasted veggies will keep for up to a week in the fridge.

Alice Zaslavsky

Leftover Veggie Salad
with Brown Rice

Serves 4
Prep 5 minutes

EQUIPMENT
Large mixing bowl

INGREDIENTS

2 cups cooked brown rice (see page 44), cooled slightly

2 cups roasted vegetables (see page 191), cooled slightly

3 cloves roasted garlic (see page 191)

½ lemon

olive oil

salt flakes

a handful of flat-leaf parsley (optional)

1 Place the brown rice and roasted vegetables in the large mixing bowl and toss together gently.

2 Squeeze the roasted garlic out of its skin into a small bowl. Mash it, then squeeze over the lemon and add a good slug of olive oil. Stir to combine, and season with salt to taste.

3 Pour the roasted garlic dressing over the vegetables and rice, and toss to combine. Serve warm or cold. If you wish, chop the parsley leaves and sprinkle them over to garnish.

Alice Zaslavsky

Leftover Veggie Frittata

Serves 6
Prep 10 minutes
Cook 15 minutes

EQUIPMENT
oven, oven-safe frying pan, cooktop,
mixing bowl

INGREDIENTS
25 g butter
2 cups leftover roasted vegetables (see page 191)
a handful of flat-leaf parsley (optional)
8 eggs
½ cup finely grated Parmesan cheese
salt and freshly ground black pepper

1   Preheat the oven to 180°C.

2   Place the butter in the oven-safe frying
    pan over a medium heat on the cooktop,
    and allow it to melt. When it starts to
    bubble, add the roasted vegetables and
    fry for 1–2 minutes.

3   If using the parsley, chop the leaves
    finely. Place the eggs, Parmesan and
    parsley (if using) in the mixing bowl,
    and whisk together until well combined.

4   Pour the egg mixture into the pan with
    the vegetables, and stir gently to combine.
    Place the pan in the oven for 15 minutes
    or until the egg mixture is just set, with
    a slight wobble in the middle. Season
    with salt and pepper to taste, and serve
    immediately.

Alice Zaslavsky

Leftover Veggie Soup

Serves 4
Prep 5 minutes
Cook 10 minutes

EQUIPMENT
blender, saucepan, cooktop

INGREDIENTS
2 cups leftover roasted vegetables (see page 191)
2 cups chicken or vegetable stock
salt flakes
freshly ground black pepper
olive oil
a handful of flat-leaf parsley (optional)

1 Place the roasted vegetables and stock in the blender and blitz to your desired texture.

2 Pour the blitzed vegetables into the saucepan and bring to a simmer over a medium heat. Season to taste with salt and pepper, and serve with a few drops of olive oil drizzled on top. If desired, chop the parsley leaves and sprinkle them over to garnish.

Stefano Manfredi

Minestrone

Serves 6
Prep 10 minutes
Cook 50 minutes

EQUIPMENT
vegetable peeler (optional),
heavy-bottomed soup pot, cooktop

INGREDIENTS

2 brown onions
8 cloves garlic
2 large carrots
1 celery heart, including
   the light-green leaves
¼ small white cabbage
300 g can of whole peeled
   tomatoes
4–5 leaves cavolo nero
   (Tuscan kale)
400 g waxy potatoes
½ bunch flat-leaf parsley
¼ cup extra virgin olive oil

2 bay leaves
salt flakes
300 g can of borlotti beans
   (cannellini or butter
   beans also work)
60 g Parmesan rind,
   wax scraped off with
   a sharp knife
freshly grated Parmesan
   cheese, to serve
freshly ground black
   pepper
crusty bread, to serve

Monty says:
This soup is great the day it is made, but
even better the next.

1 Prepare the vegetables:
   · Trim the tops off the onions and cut
     each in half through the root. Remove
     the dry layers of skin, then chop each
     half into dice, discarding the root.
   · Trim the bottoms off the garlic cloves,
     remove the skin and chop the garlic
     into slices and then smallish pieces.
   · Peel the carrot, trim off both ends and
     cut the carrot in half lengthways. Cut
     each half into three or four long pieces
     and then into dice.
   · Roughly chop the celery and cabbage,
     keeping them separate. You want
     2 cups of chopped cabbage.
   · Tip the canned tomatoes into a bowl
     and mash them with a fork.
   · Remove the stalks from the cavolo
     nero and roughly chop the leaves.
   · Peel the potatoes, then cut them into
     thickish slices. Cut the slices into
     strips and then dice.
   · Pick the leaves off the stems of parsley
     and chop them roughly.

TIP
This soup uses
Parmesan rind cut up into
small pieces. It's delicious
because it melts but retains
a little 'chewiness'.

2   Heat the olive oil in the soup pot over a medium-high heat. Add the chopped onion, garlic, carrot, celery heart and bay leaves. Stir regularly until the onion starts to soften and become translucent.

3   Add the cabbage and lightly fry the vegetables for 2–3 minutes, stirring regularly to make sure they don't colour. Add in a good pinch or two of salt and stir to combine. Once the cabbage starts to become translucent, add the canned tomatoes and stir to combine.

4   Add about 1 cup of water to bring the ingredients together, then add the cavolo nero, potatoes and beans, and stir to combine. Cover the ingredients with water (about 4 cups). Bring the soup to the boil, then turn the heat down to medium-low and simmer. Add a couple of good pinches of salt and stir. Keep simmering for 30 minutes until the vegetables are tender.

5   Chop the scraped Parmesan rind into ½ cm cubes. When the vegetables are tender, add the Parmesan rind and parsley to the pot and simmer for another 10 minutes. Turn off the heat, adjust the seasoning with salt and freshly ground pepper, and serve with plenty of grated Parmesan and crusty bread.

Neil Perry

Pan-fried Crispy-skin Hapuka

Serves 4
Prep 10 minutes
Cook 8 minutes

EQUIPMENT
paper towel, 2 large frying pans
(one should be stainless steel or
steel, not non-stick), cooktop

INGREDIENTS

¼ bunch each of several
herbs (e.g. coriander,
parsley, mint, dill,
tarragon)
1 small French shallot
2 spring onions
4 hapuka fillets
(180 g each), skin on

1 tablespoon vegetable oil
2 tablespoons extra virgin
olive oil
juice of ½–1 lemon
sea salt and freshly ground
black pepper
1 lemon

1   Prepare the salad vegetables:
   · Roughly chop the herbs — you want
     1 cup in total. Place all the chopped
     herbs together in a bowl.
   · Trim the top off the shallot and cut
     it in half through the root. Remove
     the dry layers of skin, then finely
     slice each half lengthways and add
     it to the bowl.
   · Trim the spring onions and remove
     the outer layer of skin. Finely slice the
     spring onions into rounds and add
     them to the bowl.

TIP
You can use other fish in
place of hapuka. Snapper is
a particular favourite.

2 Place the fish fillets on a board, skin-side up. Run the blade of a chopping knife carefully along the skin to scrape the moisture off and blot dry with a paper towel. Repeat this about four times — a dry skin makes for crispness.

3 Put a large stainless steel or steel frying pan on the stove, add the vegetable oil and heat until the oil is just smoking. Place the fish in, skin-side down, then place another pan on top and apply pressure. You can also use a large saucepan partly filled with water to apply the pressure — just make sure it's large enough to press down on all of the fish. If you don't have a large enough pan to hand, use a fish slice.

4 Cook while applying pressure for about 5 minutes, until the skin is crisp, then remove the top pan, turn the fish and cook (with no pressure) for about 3 minutes on the other side. Remove from the heat and place on a plate to rest for 1 minute while you finish the salad.

5 Mix together the herbs, shallot and spring onion. Just before serving, add the extra virgin olive oil, lemon juice and some seasoning and toss to combine. Cut the lemon into wedges and set aside.

6 Place a fillet of fish on each plate and place a good amount of salad next to it, sprinkle with extra salt and pepper, and serve with a lemon wedge.

TIP
You can use pretty
much anything you like.
Good options include frozen
berries, toasted nuts or
any chopped fresh or
dried fruit.

Tom Walton

Banana-flavoured
Overnight Oats

Serves 8
Prep 5 minutes
+ overnight

EQUIPMENT
mixing bowl, container with lid
(or use plastic wrap to cover the
container)

INGREDIENTS
1 large ripe banana
 (or 2 smaller ones)
1½ cups rolled oats
1 cup milk
1 cup natural Greek
 yoghurt
2 teaspoons ground
 cinnamon
3 tablespoons honey or
 maple syrup, plus extra
 to serve

Topping ideas
We used:
· sultanas
· walnuts
· strawberries
· dried cranberries
· shredded coconut
· peanut butter

Tom says:
Overnight oats are one of the most no-fuss,
do-ahead breakfasts around — they're
incredibly simple to make! Just mix together
the ingredients in a glass jar or plastic
container at night, pop them in the fridge,
and your breakfast will be ready as soon as
you wake up. Quantities can be increased
to make more. Easy-peasy! Use any milk
depending on your preference: coconut,
almond and regular cow's milk are all
great options.

1   Peel the banana, place it in the mixing
    bowl or container and mash it with
    a fork.

2   Add the remaining ingredients except for
    the toppings, and mix well. If the mixture
    looks a little dry, you can add more milk
    or yoghurt. Cover with plastic wrap or the
    container lid, and refrigerate overnight.

3   In the morning, give the oat mixture
    a good stir. Spoon one serve into a bowl
    (or container, if you're on the go), then
    finish by adding your favourite toppings.

TIP
You can also use dried dates — just soak them in warm water for 1 hour before using them. Medjool dates are quite large, so double the number if using small dried dates.

Tom Walton

Powerballs

Serves 10–12
Prep 10 minutes

EQUIPMENT
Blender

INGREDIENTS
12 Medjool dates
½ cup peanut or almond butter
¾ cup LSA (linseed, sunflower and almond meal) or almond meal
2 tablespoons cocoa powder
1½ cups desiccated coconut (used in 2 lots)
a pinch of salt

Tom says:
Powerballs are really easy and quick to make, and are a fantastic grab-and-go snack to have on the run at any time of the day. They can also be thrown into a blender with the milk of your choice to make a quick and nutritious smoothie — try 3 powerballs to ½ cup milk and adjust to suit your taste. If you don't have a blender, just chop the dates as finely as you can, and mix everything together with your hands.

1 Remove the pits (stones) from the dates and place them in a blender. Add the peanut butter or almond butter, LSA or almond meal, cocoa, half the coconut and a good pinch of salt.

2 Blitz to combine, scraping down the sides every so often. If the mixture is a little dry, add 1 tablespoon of water, then blitz again. Repeat if necessary, until the mixture starts to stick together. Scrape the mixture out into a bowl.

3 Place the remaining coconut on a large plate or a board. Spoon out a heaped tablespoon of mixture and roll it into a ball with your hands, then roll the ball in the coconut. Repeat with the remaining mixture.

4 Store in an airtight container in the fridge until you're ready to head out the door. They will keep for 1-2 weeks.

Feed an Army

Miguel Maestre

Paella
à la Maestre

Serves 4
Prep 10–15 minutes
Cook 30 minutes

EQUIPMENT
food processor (optional), large (30 cm) frying pan or paella pan, cooktop

INGREDIENTS

Sofrito base
2 large ripe tomatoes
2 large roasted red capsicums from a jar (piquillo peppers)
2 cloves garlic
½ bunch chives
½ bunch parsley

2 chicken breasts or thighs
2 chorizo sausages
2½ tablespoons good-quality extra virgin olive oil

1 teaspoon saffron threads
1 tablespoon smoked paprika
2 cups chicken stock
200 g (about 1 cup) Bomba rice (short-grain paella rice)
50 g (⅓ cup) fresh or frozen peas
salt and freshly ground black pepper
1 lemon

Miguel says:
If you are feeding a bigger crowd, just scale up the recipe. You might need a second pan!

1 Prepare the ingredients for the sofrito:
   • Cut the tomatoes in half, remove the tough green stem and chop the tomatoes roughly.
   • Trim the bottoms off the garlic cloves and remove the skin.
   • Trim the long stems off the parsley and discard.

2 Place all the sofrito ingredients in the food processor and process until chunky. If you don't have a food processor, then simply roughly chop the tomatoes and capsicums and finely chop the garlic, chives and parsley. Set aside.

TIP
Sofrito is a sauce made by frying finally sliced vegetables. It is the soul of a good paella.

3 Cut the chicken into 2 cm wide strips and then into 2 cm dice. If the chorizo sausages have a thick, papery skin, remove this. Cut the chorizo into small chunks, about half the size of the chicken pieces.

4 Preheat the large frying pan or paella pan over a medium-high heat. Add the oil, chicken and chorizo and cook for about 5 minutes, stirring occasionally, until golden-brown. Once the meat is lightly browned (but not fully cooked), remove it from the heat and set it aside on a plate.

5 Add the sofrito base to the pan, along with the saffron and paprika. Cook for 3-4 minutes, until the tomatoes start to become juicy. Add the chicken stock and bring to the boil. Stir in the rice, then return the chicken and chorizo to the pan. Leave to simmer over a medium heat for 15 minutes (avoid stirring while the stock reduces).

6 When the rice is tender and the liquid has almost fully reduced (there should still be a little liquid in the pan), check to see if a 'soccarrada' (crust) has formed on the bottom of the pan.

7 Once you see the soccarrada, your paella is ready. Turn off the heat, add the peas and leave them in the pan for another 5 minutes — the residual heat of the pan will be enough to cook the peas.

8 Season to taste with salt and pepper. Cut thick slices off the sides of the lemon (these are lemon cheeks), and squeeze the juice over just before serving.

Brigitte Hafner

Beef Stew
with Red Wine & Onions

Serves 4–6
Prep 45 minutes
Cook 2 hours

EQUIPMENT
oven, large and heavy-based
casserole pot, cooktop

INGREDIENTS
1 kg gravy beef
2 large brown onions
1 clove garlic
400 g can of whole peeled
　tomatoes
olive oil
salt and freshly ground
　black pepper

2 bay leaves (I prefer fresh)
a sprig of rosemary
250 ml (1 cup) red wine
250 ml (1 cup) chicken
　stock (a made-up stock
　cube will do)

1　Preheat the oven to 165°C.

2　Prepare the ingredients:
- Cut the beef into thick strips and then large dice.
- Trim the tops off the onions and cut each in half through the root. Remove the dry layers of skin, then chop each onion half into dice, discarding the root.
- Trim the bottom off the garlic clove, remove the skin and chop the garlic into thin slices and then small pieces.
- Tip the canned tomatoes into a bowl. Pick out the tomatoes, chop them roughly into dice and return them to the bowl.

TIP
This casserole can easily be cooked in advance; in fact, it's even better the next day. If there are any leftovers, you can break up the meat and toss it through pasta.

3   Heat a large, heavy-based casserole pot on the cooktop
    over a medium-high heat, and add enough oil to just
    cover the bottom. Add a handful of the meat and fry it
    until browned on all sides, being careful not to overcrowd
    the pot — you want your pieces of beef to go nice and
    brown, and not stew in their own juices. As each batch
    browns, transfer it to a bowl.

4   Once all the beef has been browned, you should have
    a pot that has a crusty-brown bottom. Add a good dash
    of olive oil to this, then add the onions and a sprinkle of
    salt and pepper. Cook over a medium heat, stirring until
    the onions have gone soft; the brown bits will start to
    come up off the bottom of the pot. When the onions are
    soft, turn the heat up and cook until they are a deep
    golden-brown. All up this might take about 10–15 minutes.

5   Now add your garlic, tomatoes, bay leaves, sprig of
    rosemary and the browned beef plus any juices that
    have come out. Add the red wine and cook for about
    5 minutes, until it has reduced a bit. Stir to make sure
    all the brown bits on the bottom are scraped off and
    mixed in.

6   Now add the stock, cover with a lid and put in the
    oven for about 1½ hours. Check after 1 hour — the
    meat should be falling-apart soft. If it's not quite ready,
    keep cooking. Serve with anything that will soak up the
    meaty juices, such as creamy mashed potatoes, soft
    polenta or baked semolina gnocchi.

Adriano Zumbo

Chocolate Brownies

Makes about 25
Prep 15 minutes
Cook 40 minutes
+ 1–2 hours to cool

EQUIPMENT
oven, baking tin (20 cm square
or similar size), baking paper,
microwave-safe bowl + microwave
(or heatproof bowl + saucepan +
cooktop), 2 large mixing bowls,
whisk, sieve

INGREDIENTS

120 g butter, plus a little
  extra for greasing
460 g good-quality dark
  chocolate buttons
  (70% cocoa)
6 large eggs
2 cups caster sugar
½ ripe avocado
¼ cup vegetable oil

¾ cup plain flour
2 teaspoons baking powder
½ cup cocoa powder
a pinch of salt
1 cup frozen raspberries
  (optional)
150 g white chocolate
  buttons (optional)

1   Preheat the oven to 170°C. Grease the
    baking tin with butter and line it with
    baking paper, covering the bottom and
    the sides. Cut the remaining butter into
    small pieces.

2   If you have a microwave, place the
    chocolate buttons and butter in the
    microwave-safe bowl and zap for
    2 minutes on high. Stir. If the chocolate
    hasn't melted completely, return it to
    the microwave for 30 seconds on high
    and stir again. Repeat this last step if
    necessary, until melted.

    If you don't have a microwave, half-fill
    the saucepan with water. Place this over
    a medium-high heat and bring it to the
    boil, then turn the heat down until the
    water is simmering gently. Place the
    chocolate and butter in the heatproof
    bowl and place this over the water,
    making sure that the water doesn't touch
    the bottom of the bowl. Stir until the
    chocolate and butter have melted.

TIP
You could also make
these with whatever
chocolate you like, and
add chopped nuts,
raisins, popcorn, etc.

3 Place the eggs in the large mixing bowl and whisk until well combined and a little frothy. Add the sugar and whisk in until the mixture is no longer grainy.

4 Pour the chocolate mixture into the egg mixture and stir to combine.

5 Scoop the avocado flesh into a separate small bowl and use a fork to mash it. Add the oil, and stir to combine. Pour the avocado mixture into the chocolate mixture, and stir to combine — there's no need to be too careful about this, just mix it more or less together.

6 Sift the flour and baking powder together into the other large mixing bowl, and sift the cocoa. Add the flour and cocoa to the chocolate mixture in three or four batches, mixing to incorporate each time. Stir in a good pinch of salt, then fold in the raspberries and white chocolate, if using.

7 Pour the brownie batter into the lined tin and bake in the oven for 40 minutes. When ready, it should just be firm to the touch in the middle. Set aside in the tin to cool.

8 When fully cooled, cut into squares and serve. A few fresh raspberries served alongside look pretty.

9 Store in an airtight container for up to 3 days (if they last that long). The brownies also freeze really well, for up to 6 months. Defrost in the microwave for a warm fudgy brownie, or in the fridge if you're doing it in advance.

Conversion Tables

Common abbreviations

g	gram
kg	kilogram
oz	ounce
lb	pound
mm	millimetre
cm	centimetre
in	inch
ml	millilitre
L	litre
fl oz	fluid ounce
tsp	teaspoon
dsp	dessertspoon
tbsp	tablespoon
°C	degrees Celsius
°F	degrees Fahrenheit

Weight conversions

Metric	Imperial
15 g	½ oz
30 g	1 oz
60 g	2 oz
90 g	3 oz
100 g	3½ oz
125 g	4½ oz
150 g	5 oz
200 g	7 oz
250 g	9 oz
300 g	10½ oz
350 g	12½ oz
400 g	14 oz
450 g	16 oz (1 lb)
500 g	18 oz
1 kg	36 oz (2¼ lb)

Length conversions

Metric	Imperial
0.5 cm (5 mm)	¼ in
1 cm	½ in
2.5 cm	1 in
5 cm	2 in
7.5 cm	3 in
10 cm	4 in
12.5 cm	5 in
15 cm	6 in
18 cm	7 in
20 cm	8 in
23 cm	9 in
25½ cm	10 in
28 cm	11 in
30 cm	12 in (1 foot)
40 cm	16 in

Cup & spoon conversions

Spoon/cup	Metric
½ tsp	2.5 ml
1 tsp	5 ml
1 dsp	10 ml
1 tbsp (4 tsp)*	20 ml*
⅛ cup	30 ml
¼ cup	65 ml
1/3 cup	85 ml
½ cup	125 ml
2/3 cup	170 ml
¾ cup	190 ml
1 cup	250 ml
1½ cups	375 ml
2 cups	500 ml
4 cups	1 L

Oven temperatures

Celsius	Fahrenheit	Gas mark	Description
110°C	225°F	¼	very low/cool
120°C	250°F	½	very low/cool
140°C	275°F	1	low/cool
150°C	300°F	2	low/cool
170°C	325°F	3	medium/moderate
180°C	350°F	4	medium/moderate
190°C	375°F	5	moderate-hot
200°C	400°F	6	moderate-hot
220°C	425°F	7	high/hot
230°C	450°F	8	high/hot
240°C	475°F	9	very hot
260°C	500°F	10	very hot

* This is unique to Australia; in most other parts of the world, 1 tbsp is 15 ml (3 tsp).

Contributors

Mark Best
Mark Best didn't grow up with the dream of becoming a chef — he was an electrician in the Kalgoorlie mines until the age of 25, when he started his cooking apprenticeship. Mark later opened one of Sydney's most respected fine-dining restaurants, Marque, where he was the chef and owner for 12 years. In 2010, Marque was called the 'breakthrough restaurant' on the World's 50 Best Restaurants list, and Mark was named chef of the year by the *Sydney Morning Herald*. He was also awarded Restaurant of the Year in 2011.

Martin Boetz
Born in Germany and raised in Australia, Martin Boetz has firmly established himself as our local Thai food master. After leaving school to complete his cooking apprenticeship, he worked as a chef in a number of high-end Australian restaurants before landing the job of executive chef at Longrain, a restaurant regarded as propelling Thai cuisine into the spotlight. After 13 years, he pulled up stumps to become a farmer and is now the creator and owner of Cooks Co-op, where he grows vegetable produce to supply some of Sydney's top restaurants.

Bernard Chu
Bernard Chu's grandparents owned a Malaysian bakery — and so for Bernard, pastries and desserts are in his blood. Starting out as an apprentice at one of Kuala Lumpur's five-star hotels, Bernard then moved to Sydney to study pâtisserie. Now in his mid-twenties, Bernard is the chef and co-owner of LuxBite, one of Melbourne's premier patisseries. LuxBite is known for its Asian-inspired creations, bold colours and incredible flavours.

Jill Dupleix
Jill Dupleix 'wrote the book' on Aussie food. Not only has she held the post of food editor at a number of Sydney and Melbourne publications, but Dupleix and her food critic husband, Terry Durack, have also edited a popular Australian food guide together for six years. When Jill isn't writing, she can be found eating her way around the world, presenting and speaking at food summits and spending time in the Victorian countryside where she grew up.

Anna Eoclidi
Anna Eoclidi is the heart and mind behind Pasta Emilia, one of Sydney's favourite pasta restaurants. She grew up making pasta from scratch in her home town of Emilia in Italy and is inspired by the slow food and organic movement, using only local, organic ingredients in her restaurants.

Colin Fassnidge
This infamous celebrity chef began his career in some of London's most prestigious restaurants before deciding to combine his love of travel with work and heading to Australia. He worked as executive chef at Four in Hand, one of Sydney's most acclaimed restaurants. In 2011 he opened his own restaurant, 4Fourteen, which was awarded a chef's hat just four months after its doors opened. He is a champion of nose-to-tail cooking and to him, secondary cuts may be even better than the best.

Sarah Glover
Born into a family of eight children in Tasmania, Sarah Glover comes from a long line of creatives, and has combined this natural gift with her passion for cooking. After getting her start in the hospitality industry at the age of 16, she has become an industry expert, helping to design menus for restaurants and cafés in Sydney, the Gold Coast and New York.

Analiese Gregory
After growing up in rural parts of Australia and New Zealand, Analiese Gregory moved on to work in some of the world's most prestigious restaurants, including Quay, Mugaritz and Michel Bras. Her talent for cooking has translated into a talent for creating, culminating in the launch of Bar Brosé, her very own offering to the trendy Darlinghurst neighbourhood in Sydney.

Brigitte Hafner
Australian chef Brigitte Hafner is the co-owner of Gertrude Street Enoteca, a popular wine bar and eatery in Melbourne's inner suburb of Fitzroy. Her style is simple and soulful, with an emphasis on seasonal and locally sourced produce. Brigitte has written a weekly recipe column for Melbourne's *The Age* newspaper, and she is a regular contributor to several national food magazines.

Dan Hong
Dan Hong is one of the characters of Sydney's cooking scene, and has a sneaker collection to rival the best. Starting his apprenticeship in hotels, he went on to perfect his skills at a number of leading Sydney restaurants before winning the 2008 Josephine Pignolet Young Chef of the Year award. Dan is the executive chef across a number of Sydney restaurants for high-profile restaurant group Merivale, and his obsessive love of big flavours and indulgent eating has earned him a reputation for bold food experiences. He has published his own cookbook and starred in a popular television cooking show.

Monty Koludrovic
Raised on the far north coast of New South Wales, Monty got his break in the cooking world at a small café in Byron Bay. After training and working throughout Europe and then heading up the kitchen at acclaimed Australian restaurant Bécasse, he became head chef at the iconic Icebergs, perched on the cliffs at Bondi Beach. Inspired by his Russian nonna's huge family feasts, Monty is all about sourcing the highest quality seasonal ingredients to create amazing food experiences.

Mark LaBrooy
Born in Goulburn to Sri Lankan and Swedish parents, Mark has been cooking since the age of 18. He completed his apprenticeship at Sydney restaurant Tetsuya's, known as a training ground for some of Australia's best chefs. Mark then spent seven years travelling around the world, surfing and cooking. On returning home in 2010, Mark and two of his chef mates opened their first restaurant, Three Blue Ducks. It became an overnight success thanks to its honest, grass-roots approach to food. In 2015, Mark and his co-owners opened The Farm in Byron Bay, which has become a major food destination for both tourists and locals.

Gregory Llewellyn
New York native Gregory Llewellyn began cooking when he was just 15. He trained and worked in the USA, opening several restaurants in his home country before moving to Sydney with his Aussie wife, Naomi. After working as the executive sous chef at a successful Sydney restaurant, Gregory took a sabbatical to open his own establishment with Naomi. The couple now own and operate Hartsyard, a favourite Newtown eatery that is known for its classic American menu and seasonal ingredients. Gregory has also written a cookbook.

Miguel Maestre
Born in Spain and trained in Scotland, Miguel is known as the television king of Spanish cooking in Australia. Since moving to Sydney, he has worked in some of the city's most respected kitchens. His dynamic energy has propelled him into television, where he regularly inspires home cooks to add a little spice and fun into the way they cook.

Christine Manfield
Christine Manfield is Australia's spice queen. A highly regarded chef and restaurateur with more than 20 years of experience behind her, Christine is the author of multiple award-winning cookbooks, has her own spice collection and hosts regular culinary tours around the world.

Stefano Manfredi
Born in Northern Italy, Stefano Manfredi is the last word in Italian food. A multi-award-winning chef, restaurateur, coffee blender, cookbook author and food writer, Stefano has changed the way Italian food is perceived in Australia. He is an outspoken ambassador of food sustainability, and has opened high-end dining establishments in Sydney and on the New South Wales central coast.

Lillia McCabe
A Hot Talent nominee for the *Time Out* Sydney Food Awards 2016, Lillia McCabe is currently wowing Sydney foodies with her cooking at ACME, a one-hat restaurant located in Sydney's Rushcutters Bay.

Monday Morning Cooking Club
Originally getting together to write a cookbook to raise money for charity, the six women who make up the sisterhood of the Monday Morning Cooking Club have now been cooking together every Monday morning since 2006. With two cookbooks and an impressive number of loyal followers scattered across the globe, the sisterhood's mission is to share the Jewish community's passion and connection to food with Australia.

Josh Niland
To say that Josh Niland is passionate about fish would be to put it too lightly. After cutting his teeth at popular restaurants Ananas Bar and Brasserie and Est., he decided to open his own homage to all things fish — Saint Peter, in the lush surroundings of Sydney's Paddington.

Mitch Orr
Mitch Orr has come a long way from studying food tech in high school — a 2010 Josephine Pignolet Young Chef of the Year, he honed his craft at the prestigious Sepia, and now runs his own successful restaurant, ACME in Rushcutters Bay.

Neil Perry
Neil Perry is one of Australia's most influential chefs and food industry icons. Obsessed with doing things the right way, not the easy way, Neil is a huge fan of Asian cuisine and can often be found in noodle bars and hawker stalls around the world, looking for his next best meal. Over the years, Neil has owned and run several high-profile restaurants across Australia. He also consults for airline Qantas on their first-class and business-class menus.

Giovanni Pilu

Chef, writer and successful restaurateur Giovanni Pilu gave Sydney its introduction to Sardinian cuisine. Since moving to Australia to be with his wife and eventual business partner, Marilyn, he has opened a number of successful Sydney restaurants. Giovanni has also released an award-winning cookbook and established himself as a founding member and president of the Council of Italian Restaurants in Australia.

Anthony Puharich

Anthony Puharich is one of Australia's leading butchers and entrepreneurs. A fifth-generation butcher, Anthony connects the best meat producers in Australia with the best chefs. His flagship store, Victor Churchill in Sydney's Woollahra, has won international interior design awards for bringing glamour and high design to butchery, and has become a destination for international celebrities and food royalty.

Hayden Quinn

Hayden Quinn grew up on Sydney's northern beaches, and when he wasn't surfing he could be found in the kitchen. An appearance on a reality cooking show propelled him further into the world of food in 2011, and that's when the fun really began. Fast-forward to 2016, and Hayden's much-loved grass-roots style of cooking has led him to front his own television series and publish a cookbook.

Katherine Sabbath

Katherine Sabbath first began baking in high school, making sweet treats for her friends. A former school teacher, Sabbath is completely self-taught. Her amazing creations have built up a social media following of nearly 110,000 people, and she is steadily feeding her reputation as Australia's queen of cakes.

Nathan Sasi

Nathan Sasi was destined for culinary greatness, showing great promise during his cooking apprenticeship. He took on roles at some of Sydney's most prestigious restaurants, followed by a stint in London and a year as the head chef at Sydney restaurant and winery Nomad. In 2015, Nathan opened Mercado, a joint venture with the team behind China Doll restaurant in Woolloomooloo.

Justine Schofield

After making it to the finals of a reality cooking show in 2009, Justine began a catering business and established herself as one of Australia's favourite home cooks. She now travels between Sydney and Melbourne for private functions and cooking-show appearances. Justine has also hosted her own television programme, *Everyday Gourmet*, since 2011. The show aims to inspire viewers to create great food at home.

Jake Smyth

From his humble beginnings in a local McDonald's at the age of 14, Jake Smyth has led a burger revolution in Sydney, opening burger joint Mary's with his partner-in-crime, Kenny Graham. Since launching in 2013, Mary's has grown into a 10,000-burgers-a-week cult favourite. Jake has also opened the Unicorn Hotel, bringing his rock-and-roll attitude to the classic Aussie pub.

Tom Walton

Tom Walton's food philosophy is all about healthy, seasonal and sustainable cooking. Growing up in the Blue Mountains of New South Wales, Tom began work at a two-hat restaurant at the age of just 17. He has represented Australia in cookery competitions around the world, and is now the head chef and owner of The Bucket List, one of Sydney's best-loved beachfront restaurants and bars.

Jemma Whiteman

The co-owner of Good Luck Pinbone in Kensington, Jemma Whiteman's professional history reads like a who's who of Sydney's finest restaurants. She cut her teeth at Three Blue Ducks, Berta and Billy Kwong before moving on to open her own restaurant with partner Mike Eggbert. Good Luck Pinbone serves up innovative and creative food that's accessible to the masses.

Daniel Wilson

Daniel Wilson knows all there is to know about burgers. A New Zealand native, he had decided he wanted to be a chef by the age of 12. After training in the USA, Daniel moved to Melbourne, where he became head chef at a series of restaurants. He was the driving force behind the Fitzroy restaurant Huxtable, which was recognised with a chef's hat in 2014. Daniel now co-owns and runs the hugely successful burger chain Huxtaburger.

Alice Zaslavsky

After studying for a Bachelor of Teaching at Melbourne University, Alice's career as a teacher went on hold when she found herself appearing on a reality cooking show in 2012. Alice is the author of a best-selling children's cookbook and is also the food editor for *The Weekly Review*, a popular Melbourne news publication. When she's not writing, you'll find Alice hosting cooking shows for children on television.

Adriano Zumbo

One of Australia's most celebrated pâtissiers, Adriano Zumbo has firmly established himself as our king of desserts. After becoming a household name thanks to his incredible creations on numerous popular cooking programmes, Adriano now has nine stores throughout New South Wales and Victoria, as well as two cookbooks and two television series under his belt.

INDEX

Page numbers in italics within the recipe section refer to photographs.

Acknowledgements & Credits

The publisher would like to give special thanks to Helen Greenwood for sparking the idea for this book. We would also like to thank Matt Okine and each and every one of the chefs and food writers who contributed recipes; may your tips, tricks and wisdom inspire budding chefs for years to come. Huge thanks to Jason Loucas, who so beautifully captured each of the contributors with unfailing grace and humour. Thanks also to Jason Marshall, who leapt in at the eleventh hour to consult. And finally, thank you to the team at ABC, especially Richard Huddleston, James Peyton and Lisa Hunter. We most certainly couldn't have done it without you.

For PQ Blackwell

Publisher: Geoff Blackwell
Editor-in-chief: Ruth Hobday
Design: Cameron Gibb
Additional design: Helene Dehmer
Project editor: Leanne Mcgregor
Copy editor: Teresa Mcintyre
Additional editorial: Rachel Clare, Susan Brookes

For ABC TV

Head of entertainment: Jon Casimir
Executive producer: Richard Huddleston
Series producer and director: James Peyton
Director: Dave Wallace
Editors: Richard Holz and Campbell Wilson
Principal photography: Phil Dow and Richard Berrill
Sound: Jason Dirckze
Production manager: Gannon Conroy
Production co-ordinator: Kirra Homer
Production assistant: Aimee Lili-Peters
Researchers: Melissa Leong, Tammi Kwok and Jane Grylls
With special thanks to: Alice Zaslavsky

Short Cuts to Glory is an ABC TV Entertainment production. Based on an original idea by Helen Greenwood.

echo

Echo Publishing
An imprint of Bonnier Publishing Australia
Level 6, 534 Church Street, Richmond
Victoria 3121 Australia
bonnierpublishing.com.au
Facebook: facebook.com/bonnierpublishingau
Twitter: @bonnierau
Instagram: instagram.com/bonnierpublishingau

Produced and originated by PQ Blackwell Limited, Suite 405 IronBank, 150 Karangahape Road, Auckland 1010, New Zealand, pqblackwell.com

A Cataloguing-in-Publication entry is available from the catalogue of the National Library of Australia at www.nla.gov.au.

ISBN: 978-1-76040-572-4
Printed in China by International Color Art Printing (Hong Kong) Co., Limited
10 9 8 7 6 5 4 3 2 1

abc.net.au/shortcuts
Instagram: @mattokine
#shortcutstoglory